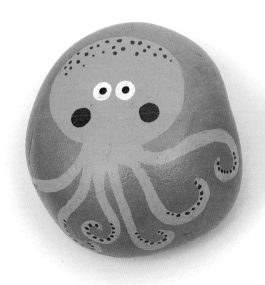

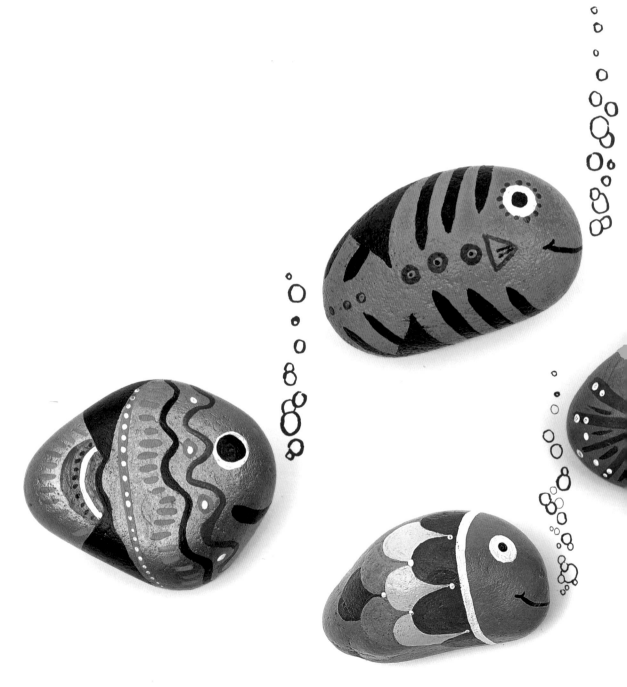

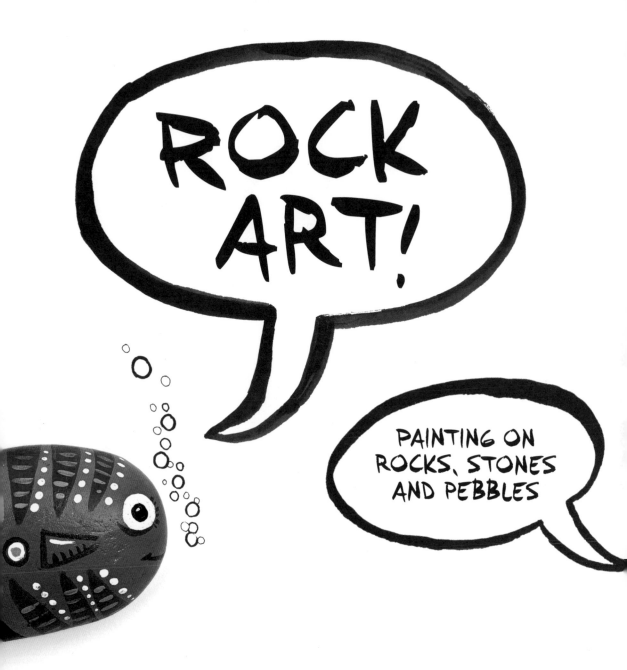

ROCK ART!

PAINTING ON ROCKS, STONES AND PEBBLES

Denise Scicluna

Search Press

A QUARTO BOOK

Published in 2015 by
Search Press Ltd
Wellwood
North Farm Road
Tunbridge Wells
Kent TN2 3DR

Reprinted 2017, 2018
Copyright © 2015 Quarto plc

ISBN: 978-1-78221-183-9

Conceived, designed and produced by
Quarto Publishing plc
The Old Brewery
6 Blundell Street
London N7 9BH

QUAR.ORAT

Senior editor: Lily de Gatacre
Senior art editor: Emma Clayton
Copy editor: Clare Sayer
Proofreader: Liz Jones
Designer: Austin Taylor
Photographer: Phil Wilkins
Illustrator: Jessica Wilson
Indexer: Helen Snaith
Art director: Caroline Guest
Creative director: Moira Clinch

Publisher: Paul Carslake

Colour separation in Hong Kong by
Bright Arts Ltd
Printed in China by 1010 Printing Limited

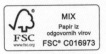

MIX
Papir iz
odgovornih virov
FSC® C016973

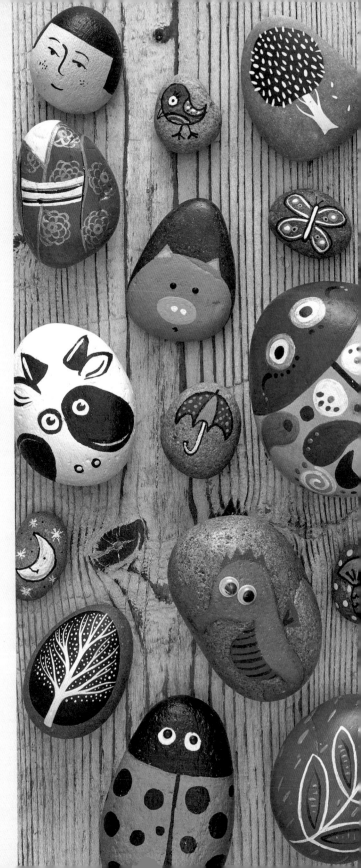

CONTENTS

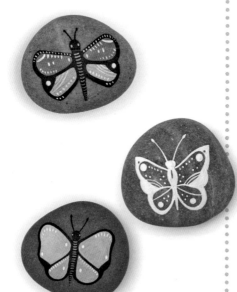

CONTENTS

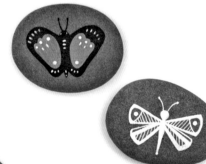

DENISE'S WORLD

'What can I do with this?' is a question that is frequently asked in the arts and crafts world, and it is then that ideas start flowing through the creative mind. It is not any different with rock art! Each pebble is unique, and this is what makes rock art exciting and fun. At times you might already have an idea of a project you want to do with your rock and can go off hunting for the perfect stone that fits the bill. Other times you can let the rock inspire you and end up creating something you never imagined. What makes all this even more enjoyable is that you do not need a lot of equipment to transform these miniature canvases! Rock art can be particularly fun for kids and totally enjoyable for adults too. It's economical and easy to get started; it really is a craft for everyone.

You'll find that your finished rock art projects can be used in practical, stylish, fun and decorative ways. Once painted, pebbles can be used as jewellery, lucky amulets, games, love tokens, bookends, special gifts or home and garden décor objects! It almost feels like magic to turn these natural rocks that most people totally ignore into little bugs, cars, flowers, feathers, owls and so many other objects and amazing creatures!

This book makes it possible for anyone to create extraordinary art projects and crafts with ordinary rocks. The first part of the book will give you tips as to how to go about picking your pebbles and how to get started. I will then guide you through the projects, all of which can be easily carried out in your home. Lastly, you will find some magical ideas for how you can use these pebbles once transformed. Don't worry if you have no or little experience with painting; this book will awaken your imagination to endless rocky and creative possibilities! Enjoy the process and do not fear getting messy.
Keep rocking!

Denise

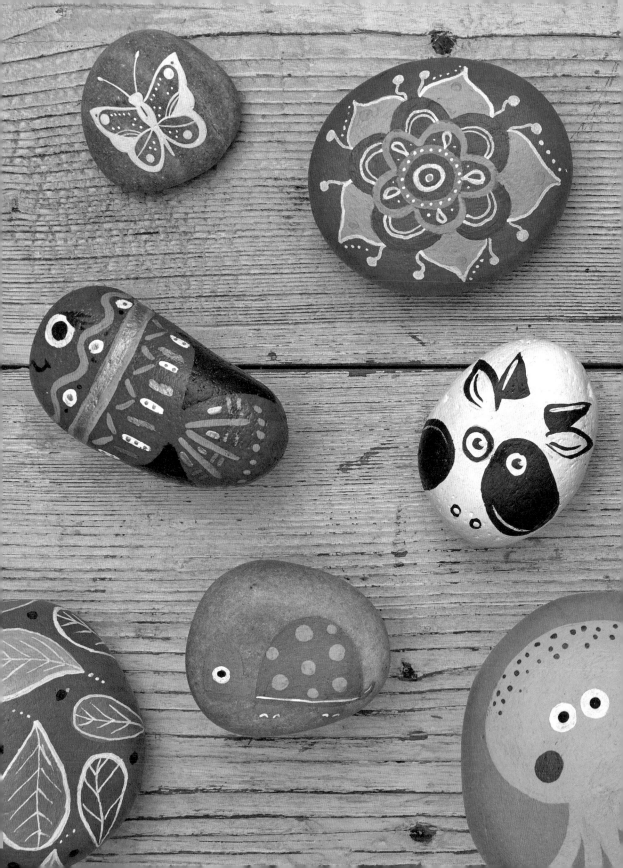

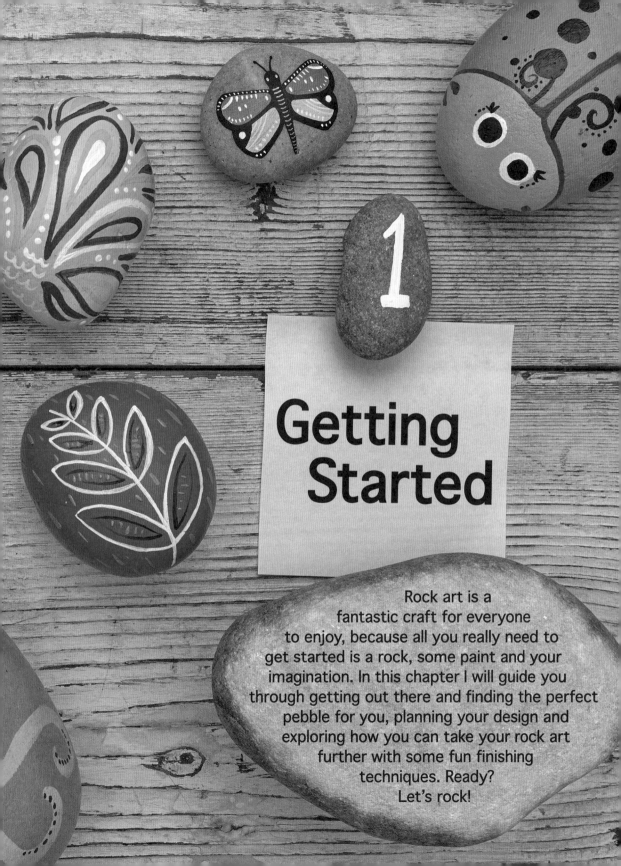

1

Getting Started

Rock art is a fantastic craft for everyone to enjoy, because all you really need to get started is a rock, some paint and your imagination. In this chapter I will guide you through getting out there and finding the perfect pebble for you, planning your design and exploring how you can take your rock art further with some fun finishing techniques. Ready?
Let's rock!

WE'RE GOING ON A ROCK HUNT

Rock painting is one of the oldest forms of expression by humankind; the earliest art form. What does all rock art have in common? A rock. It is your canvas and often your inspiration. So, the most important thing to do before you put your brush in any paint is get out there and find the rock to paint.

Notice how with a little imagination, the same design can work on vastly different shaped rocks, or even across more than one stone.

THE HUNT IS ON

Searching for the perfect stone is actually part of the fun of rock painting! How exciting is it to create endless craft projects from natural stones that you can find just outside your house or on your next nature walk by the river? You can spend hours on a beautiful beach picking out pebbles in various forms, sizes and colours. Spend just one sunny afternoon with your kids or loved ones and stock up on 'canvases' for your next 20 rock art projects. And all for free! Put your pebbles in bags or boxes, take them home with you and get ready for hours of exciting craft projects, both for adults and young ones.

IS IT A ROCK OR A PEBBLE?

Pebbles are like all other rocks and minerals. To be really specific, a pebble is actually a class of rock, larger than a granule but smaller than a cobble. What makes pebbles so beautiful are their various textures and colours. Some have lovely coloured streaks of quartz and other sedimentary rock running

through them. The various minerals in pebbles and rocks make them distinct from each other, and unique. Although generally smooth, pebbles can also be textured, which is often due to prolonged contact with seawater.

If you're not near the beach, you can also find inland pebbles along the shores of large rivers and lakes. These river pebbles are formed from river rock, as flowing water washes over particles along the shores of the rivers. The combination of soil, chemical elements and the speed of the current all impact the colour and smoothness of river pebbles. The most common colours of river rock are black, grey, green, brown and white.

It is important and helpful to have some basic knowledge of rocks and pebbles. There are three different types of rock: igneous, sedimentary and metamorphic, and they were all formed in different ways. This means they all have different appearances, properties and are found in different places. The most important thing for you is how a pebble is going to work

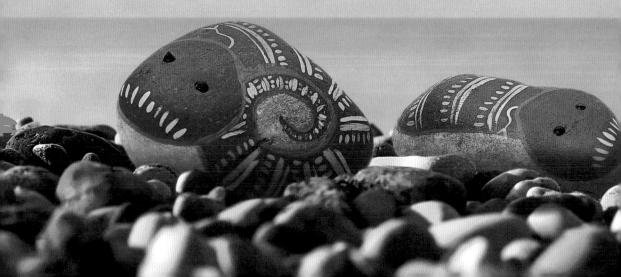

for your specific art project, but the chart on page 13 will give you some basic information about the different types of rock you will come across.

NOT UP FOR HUNTING?

Don't despair. The great news is that if you don't have the time or the inclination to go out and collect your own rocks, or you're not near to the beach or a river, you can still find your perfect rocks. Luckily, all kinds of pebbles are available to buy from craft shops, garden centres, and online.

If you are ordering pebbles online, make sure you take note of the dimensions of the pebbles so that the size will match what you have in mind. This method is very different from scanning the beach and picking the pebbles yourself, as it does not give you the chance to feel and see the pebble and let the ideas come to you. However, all online shops have available images and descriptions of the types of pebbles on sale. And of course, the major bonus of ordering online is that the stones can be delivered straight to your front door, saving you from lugging heavy rocks around with you.

When you're purchasing pebbles, prices will vary depending on what type of pebbles you are ordering; for instance pebbles with holes predrilled in them will inevitably be more expensive. Always check out at least two or three shops before making a decision, as prices can vary depending on the shop. Sometimes prices are cheaper if you purchase a big bag of pebbles – you might be lucky and get a good bulk deal. Simply pack away any unused pebbles for another project another time if you do not intend to use the whole bag.

WHAT TO LOOK FOR IN A ROCK

There are two ways that you can match up a rock with an art project: essentially you choose the project first or you choose the stone first. You might already have a certain design in mind, or a certain type of project you want to complete, that will require a specific size or shape of stone. You may have your heart set on painting a fish, an owl or a ladybird, or creating a dainty brooch or a weighty doorstop, and all of these would require a stone with different properties. The challenge then is to find just the right stone to be your canvas! Try not to be too rigid with your specifications though – think about how your design could work on various different pebble shapes. Look at the pictures at the bottom of this page. See how this snake design can work brilliantly from three different starting points. Use your imagination and you'll find new and exciting ways to bring your design to life.

If you don't already have your heart set on a design, you can simply sit back and let the pebbles you find inspire some ideas in you. Look at an interesting triangular pebble and you might see a slice of cake, a snowy mountain top or a wedge of watermelon. Turn to pages 14–15 to see how some pebbles will speak their own ideas to you and become your inspiration. Any pebble you find can be transformed into something!

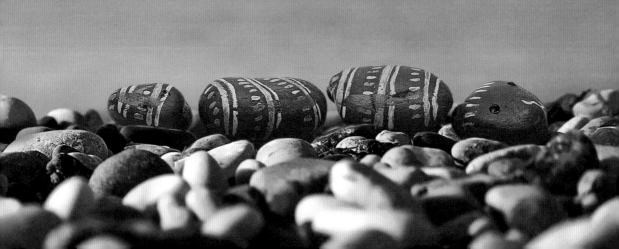

However, you need to keep some general guidelines in mind during your rock hunting. The main thing is to make sure that your pebbles have a smooth surface. Firstly, this will make it easier for you to draw with markers and pens and your linework will look neater. Secondly, a smooth, painted, and varnished surface looks much better and neater than a rough, bumpy surface, so avoid picking up rough-surfaced rocks! Every rule has an exception though, and a rough, textured stone cleaned and varnished can look wonderful displayed just on its own. Check out the examples on the right for some other general things to look out for on your hunt for that perfect pebble.

SO YOU'VE GOT THE PERFECT PEBBLE, NOW WHAT?

So now that you have found *the* pebble, what do you do with it? Where do you start? The steps and choices that follow are endless. If your pebble is small, you can make use of fine-point markers, which allow you to work in small detail and produce beautiful, intricate designs. You can choose to go for acrylic paints and paint all over your pebble, adding details with markers or a paintbrush afterwards. Outlines work beautifully in rock art – create lines and patterns on your painted pebble and add shadows to make your design stand out. Use white paint or markers on black pebbles; the effect is remarkable.

Painting pebbles can seem a little overwhelming, especially for those who have never painted before. The following pages will guide you through every step, making you feel more at ease with painting on pebbles. It offers a world of inspiration, which will hopefully bring ideas and creativity into your home and your life.

THE PERFECT ROCK

Here are some tips about what to look out for when you are searching for your perfect rock.

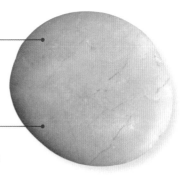

Look out for smooth surfaces. Bumps can easily distract from your design, especially if you are using marker pens rather than paint.

Pick the best side. Look out for the 'right' side of your pebble if you are painting on one side only. Often one side is more ideal and might have fewer bumps or irregularities than the other.

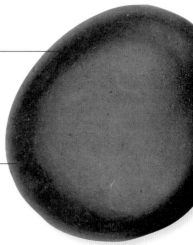

Do you plan on designing monochrome pebbles? Look out for dark and black pebbles – white painted designs will look beautiful on the dark natural texture of your pebble, and there is no need to paint a background colour.

Look out for big pebbles if you plan to work on large projects such as bookends or paperweights. Make sure they are steady, heavy and not bumpy.

Does it stand up? If you want to paint a standing pebble, test your pebble and see if it can stand. They are quite rare to find, so treasure a standing pebble!

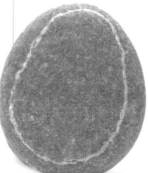
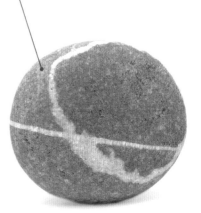

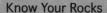

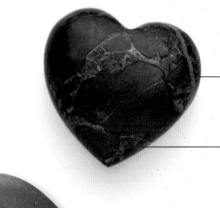

Don't be scared to pick the weird-shaped pebbles – *you might be surprised how they can inspire you!*

Get the right shape. Depending on what you plan to paint, having the right base shape will make your crafted pebbles look better. Painting a leaf? Look out for an oval rather than a circular stone.

Keep an eye out for families of pebbles. Some pebbles just seem to naturally go well together and you might want to have a project in which you include all of them, such as a set of beautiful words, matching patterns or a long snake made of three or four pebbles, like on page 11.

Special pebbles. Some pebbles have unique textures and amazing colours. Paint on your pebbles, but allow this unique colour or texture to show.

Interested in creating pebbled jewellery or accessories? Keep an eye out for tiny, smooth pebbles. Small, lightweight pebbles are the best for jewellery, magnets or brooches.

Know Your Rocks

Metamorphic Rock

Metamorphic rocks are formed when other rock types are subjected to immense heat or pressure. The movement of the Earth's plates can cause rocks to be buried and squeezed, or molten magma can cause rocks to become super-heated. The rocks do not melt, but the minerals in them undergo a chemical change and their crystals become arranged in layers. Examples include slate and marble.

Sedimentary Rock

These are formed in a more natural and prolonged way. They are formed on shores or in water by the weathering of older stones. In this weathering process, bits and pieces from older stones start to settle together with other organic materials such as parts from animals and plants. The pieces are deposited and build up into layers known as sediments and are then compacted by further layers building up on top. Examples of such rocks are sandstone, chalk, limestone and flint.

Igneous Rock

When rocks melt deep inside the earth and become molten, this is known as magma. When magma cools and solidifies, igneous rock is formed. Igneous rocks are made up of interlocking crystals in a random arrangement. The more slowly the magma cools, the bigger these crystals will be. Examples of types of igneous rock are basalt, granite and pumice.

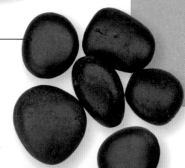

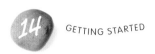

BE INSPIRED

No two rocks are identical. Look at your pebble's shape; does its form suggest a subject? You can paint just about anything on your rock canvas. Some ideas are here.

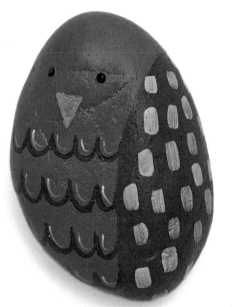

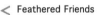

‹ Feathered Friends

It's nice to keep a painted pebble in your pocket as a talisman; this little bird will bring good luck.

Leaves ›

Pebbles offer an achievably small canvas, the perfect format for painting simplified nature subjects like leaves.

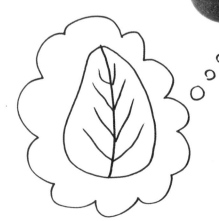

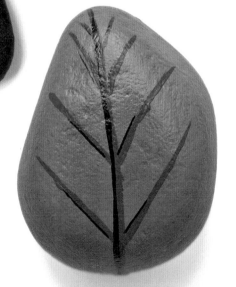

Fish

Sometimes it helps to rotate a found pebble in your hand, turn it over, and hold it in different ways to see if an idea comes to you, like the fish here.

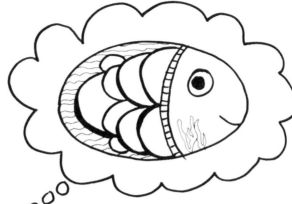

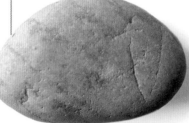

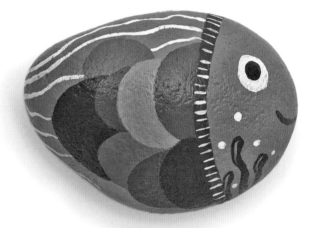

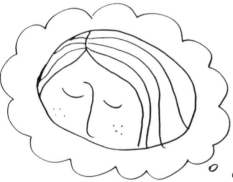

Faces

Here, the pebble's shape suggested a cheery face, but on another day, in another light, I might have used it as a canvas for a ladybird, a cloudburst or a turtle.

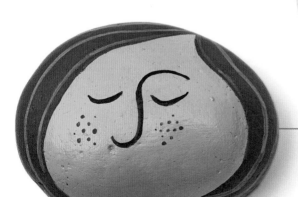

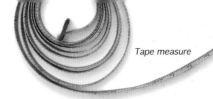

Tape measure

Pencil

Fine liner

WHAT DO YOU NEED?

The good news is that the answer is very little! As long as you've got a rock, some paint and a brush, you can get started. However, there are many tools that will prove to be really useful on your rock art journey and will enable you to save time, get better results and take your craft further. So, let's go through all the tools which you will encounter when carrying out the projects in this book.

Based on the nature of the tasks and projects, the tools below are divided into two categories. The 'must-have' tools are the bare essentials needed to paint and decorate your pebbles, and you'll find you may have many of these in your home already. The 'other' tools are for more specialised or advanced projects and using some of them can be more challenging. They help convert your pebbles into bigger projects, leading to games, accessories and house or garden decorations. Check out pages 106–123 for some great ideas!

MUST-HAVE TOOLS

Paintbrushes

It's good to have a selection so you can make use of fine brushes for outlines and details and wider ones for painting whole pebbles. Use good quality brushes and take good care of them to ensure you always get the best results.

Acrylic Craft Paint

These are the best paints to use for rock art and they come in an extraordinary range of colours so you'll always be able to find the colour you want. To begin with, rather than spashing out loads of money on paint colours you might need a tiny amount of, why not buy just the primary colours, black and white, and use them to mix any others that you want. Acrylic craft paints are reasonably priced and can be found in all arts and crafts shops.

White Chalk/Pencil

It is a good idea to outline your design before you paint and these tools are perfect for the job; use chalk on dark-coloured pebbles and pencil on light-coloured pebbles. You can always gently rub off any chalk or pencil that is still visible when you've finished painting but before you varnish.

Fine Liners

You may find it easier to use fine pens rather than paint to create detailed patterns, especially on smaller pebbles. Just make sure they are waterproof! If you are drawing over a painted area, make sure the paint is fully dry first.

Marker Pens

These come in various colours and can be used for outlining your designs and adding details if you do not want to make use of your paintbrush. If you are drawing on top of a painted area, be sure to give the paint time to completely dry first.

Varnish

An overall coat of varnish will make your finished pebbles stand out and look great. But most importantly it acts as protection and stops the paint getting bumped or chipped! You can use matt or glossy varnish depending on the look you want.

Cup of Water

Make sure you keep a cup of water nearby and use it to clean your

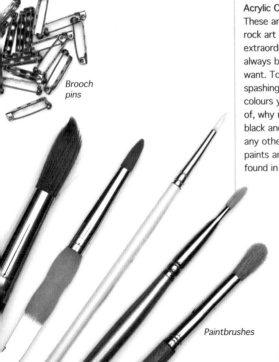

Brooch pins

Paintbrushes

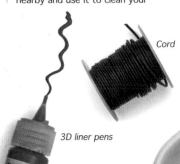

3D liner pens

Cord

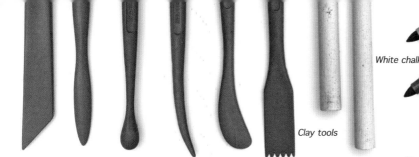

White chalk

Clay tools

Marker pens

paintbrushes between colours and when you've finished.

Paper Towels
Very useful for wiping any rogue paint from your hands, brushes and pebbles, and for quickly cleaning up any possible messes in your workspace!

Mixing Plate
Use a plastic plate to mix and add as many paint colours as you want.

Black 3D Liner Pen
These useful pens allow you to create a 3D 'blob' effect on your pebbles and are in a range of other colours. They are ideal for adding eyes and dot patterns, and great for adding a bit of textural interest to your rock art.

Hair Dryer
You can use your hair dryer to speed up the drying process. Use this if you have to wait for a small area of paint to dry before you can paint the other side or paint over it.

OTHER TOOLS
Polymer Clay
If you can't find the perfect size or shape of pebble, you can use polymer clay to create you own idea of pebble perfection. Turn to pages 18–19 to find out more about this.

Clay Tools
If you're going to use polymer clay to make your 'rocks', it is a good idea to

use a set of specialist clay tools to shape and cut the polymer clay. This will give you the best results.

Masking Tape
This would be used in a more fiddly, advanced rock art project. You can create patterns by masking out areas of the pebble and painting over the top. When the tape is (carefully!) removed, a perfectly straight stripe is created.

Brooch Pins
If you want to turn your painted pebbles into brooches or pins, you can pick up brooch pins at craft or jewellery supply shops. The best way to attach a brooch pin to a stone is to first sew the pin to a small rectangle of thick felt. You can then apply super glue to the piece of felt and securely attach this to the back of your pebble.

Chain/Cord
It's possible to turn small painted rocks into beautiful pendants. If you plan to do this, you will need a chain, some string or a cord to complete your necklace.

Rotary Tool
You can buy predrilled pebbles, but if you want to drill a hole in a pebble to turn it into a necklace or attach it to a keyring, you will need a rotary tool. Turn to page 22 for more information about this. It's crucial that you always read the manufacturer's guidelines and take all relevant safety precautions before you start.

Wood Filler
This is great to add to the bottom of a pebble to make it stand up steadily if it is too wobbly! You can also use it to add little 3D embellishments and design features to your stones. Check out page 21 for some advice on using wood filler.

Tape Measure
If you want to create really intricate designs or give your stones a professional finish, a tape measure is handy for making precise measurements for your projects.

Fabric
You might find that you need some thick felt to help attach a brooch pin or some beautifully patterned fabric to attach an appliqué motif or other design feature to a rock art project.

Glue
Whether you're adding googly eyes, brooch pins, fabric embellishments or polymer clay elements, it's a good idea to have some PVA glue and some super glue at hand.

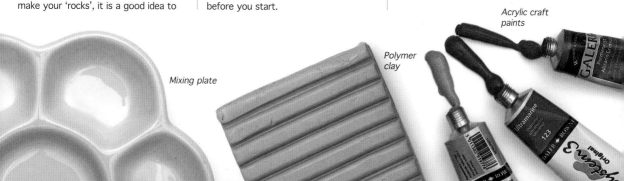

Acrylic craft paints

Polymer clay

Mixing plate

MAKE YOUR OWN ROCKS

Do you think you might not manage to find your perfect pebbles? Do you feel like being a bit more adventurous, wanting to create your own perfect pebble? Although, scientifically speaking, you won't be creating a real pebble, this challenge will give you an opportunity to truly create what you have mind. The trick is to make use of polymer clay. This is a type of modelling clay containing polyvinyl chloride (PVC). Though it doesn't actually contain real clay minerals, it is malleable and 'gel-like' to use, allowing you to give it the shape you want, and dries to something hard and solid. Polymer clay is commonly used for making arts and crafts items and decorations.

Polymer clay can be purchased in small packets of 50 g (2 oz) in a whole range of different colours, but larger packets of up 1 kg (2 lb) can also be found. There are several brands of polymer clay, which can be found in all arts and crafts shops, and are all super easy to use. Polymer clay comes in two forms: one type that is air-dried and one that needs to be baked in order to dry and harden.

WORKSPACE

The beauty of working with polymer clay is that you do not require a big space to work in. It also requires very little expense. For modelling and molding, you can work on wax paper on top of a smooth surface, or a cutting board. A marble surface is also useful as it helps keep the clay cool while it is being worked.

If you plan to make pendants out of polymer clay, you will need something with a point that is about 3 mm (⅛ inch) wide – a skewer or knitting needle would work well. This is so you can make a hole for your pendant. Push it through the clay once you have finished shaping it –

Making polymer clay pebbles

1 Take a block of polymer clay and, using a knife or blade, cut off a small piece. Remember you can go big or small – do not be scared to experiment!

2 It's time to condition your block of clay. Using your fingers and the palms of your hands, press the clay, making it softer and easier to manage. When it is smooth and soft enough, you can start creating your shape.

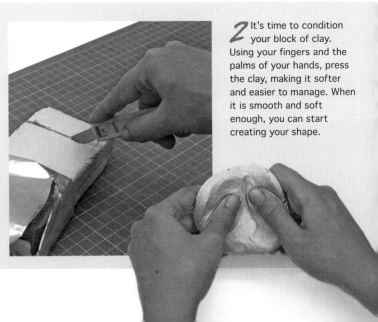

it is very important that this is done before the drying process. If you plan to be more creative, you can purchase a basic clay tool set, which will enable you to cut and engrave on your pebble. Be aware that polymer clay does contain a small amount of toxins, so it is advisable not to use kitchen utensils that are used for food preparation. A set of clay modelling tools can be used specifically for all your clay projects.

PREPARATIONS

So you have chosen your clay and your workspace is set up – what to do next? If you have no plans in mind, you can create different forms of pebbles and decide what to do with them later. In any case, it is important that the clay is conditioned before making any forms. Conditioning is the process that makes the clay ready to work with, and it is simply done by working the clay with your hand until it reaches a good working consistency. You can stretch and compress the clay and press it with your fingers. This creates a change in

the clay's texture, making it softer and more pliable. One effective way to soften and warm your piece of clay is by rolling it in your hands, creating a snake shape. Using a circular motion, press the snake back into a ball. Repeat this process several times – it should only take a few minutes. Before starting the conditioning process, you might want to put the piece of clay in a warm place for a few minutes – this can make your conditioning easier to manage.

If you are using old clay that feels dry, you can try adding some new clay to it and merging the two together. If this does not work, you can mix a few drops of mineral oil or a dab of petroleum jelly into polymer clay.

Once you feel that your clay is manageable, you can start creating your pebble forms. Create perfect round ones, flat ones or tall ones, which can be turned into a standing decoration. Make sure the surface is nice and smooth and avoid having cracks or holes, as these will still be visible even after it is covered in paint.

DRYING PROCESS

When you are happy with your form, it is now time to dry your clay. Even though air-drying clay does not take a long time, clay that is baked in the oven will produce speedier results. Your clay pebble can be baked at around 130°C (275°F) for about 15 minutes in a regular oven. It is very important to read the heating instructions that come with your pack of clay and to keep an eye on your baking clay in the oven. It is also highly recommended that you preheat the oven for some minutes before baking.

Air-drying clay can easily take up to 24 hours to harden (dry), or a bit quicker if some heat or a fan is added. This means that your pebble needs to be shaped at least a day before you plan to decorate and paint it. Putting your clay pebble next to a window can be very helpful in the drying process.

CLAY VS. REAL PEBBLES

This book is all about pebbles and rocks. However this section has shown you an edgy creative twist to rock art. It may be considered cheating, but once you see a painted rock and a painted pebble, it will be very difficult to spot the difference, unless you weigh each of them! Polymer clay is an excellent medium if you want to create a particular shape and has the added benefit of being light and easy to use.

If you are looking to show off the natural texture and colour of a rock by drawing lines and patterns on it, then avoid using polymer clay as it won't emphasise the true nature of a pebble, especially its surface and beautiful tones. However, the list of things you can create with polymer clay, just like rocks and pebbles, is endless!

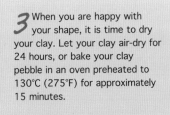

3 When you are happy with your shape, it is time to dry your clay. Let your clay air-dry for 24 hours, or bake your clay pebble in an oven preheated to 130°C (275°F) for approximately 15 minutes.

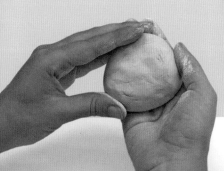

Right now the difference is easy to spot, but it'll be a different story once they're painted – unless you pick them up!

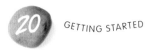

PREPARATION

The absolute first step you need to take when you've chosen your pebble is to clean it really thoroughly with a damp cloth. Then you can start to think about tweaking its shape and laying out your design.

SKETCHING YOUR IDEAS

It is well known that sketching beforehand leads to better designs – most artists make use of sketching before starting to paint. Similarly, it helps to have at least an idea of what you are about to paint on your pebble. Sketch your design in a notebook or on some paper and keep it next to you as a reference. Alternatively you can sketch the design directly on the pebbles by using chalk or pencil.

If you are using light or white pebbles, you can use a pencil to sketch your design. However, try to mark the pebble very lightly as you want to avoid having visible lines after you paint your pebble. If your pebble is darker, you can make use of chalk, which is easier to manage. The great thing about using chalk is that you can rub it off with your fingers if you make a mistake or want to start all over again.

Sketching does not mean creating an exact outline of the idea. The purpose is to have an idea of proportion and use of space on your pebble. It is a time to think about whether you are using the back or sides of the pebble, and how to organise your shapes and lines. Sketch just the basic shapes of your design; do not focus on details as ideas will start to flow once you get started with painting your pebble.

Here are some ideas and tips for those wanting to sketch their own designs. If you feel confident enough, you can easily skip this step and just go with the flow of it.

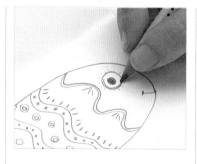

Sketching on Paper
After choosing your pebble, make a quick sketch of your design. Remember, there is no need to go into detail but feel free to present your full idea on paper. Keep the sketch next to you as you paint onto your rock.

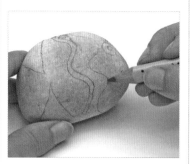

Sketching on Light Pebbles
If your pebble is white, use a pencil to make light markings of your design. Remember not to press too much to avoid having visible lines after you paint your pebble.

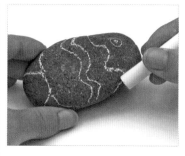

Sketching on Dark Pebbles
Using chalk, sketch your design, focusing mainly on the basic shapes. Rub out any lines with your finger if you need to. It is that easy!

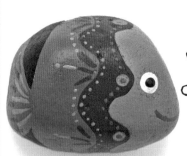

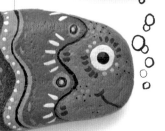

USING WOOD FILLER TO IMPROVE STRUCTURE

Upright stones can be used for figures, little sculptures or other designs that require a standing position. You might be faced with the problem of not finding the right upright stones, which can be hard to find or purchase. This problem can be solved with wood filler, a putty-like product available from hardware shops or garden centres. When sourcing wood filler, make sure you buy one that can be painted on.

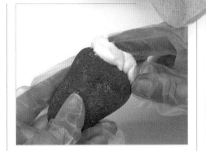

1 Wearing gloves, apply wood filler to the bottom of your pebble and smooth the filler with your fingers.

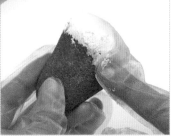

2 Blend the pebble and filler together to make it look like one piece. It might help to wet your fingers to aid the smoothing process. To dry, place your pebbles upside down, with the filler pointing up. An egg box is ideal for this process. Let them dry for at least 8 hours, by which time the pebble and the filler should be as one. Test to see if your pebble stands upright.

YOU WILL NEED

- ☑ Protected working surface
- ☑ Rubber gloves
- ☑ Wood filler
- ☑ Clean and dry pebble
- ☑ Egg box
- ☑ Medium-grade sandpaper
- ☑ White craft paint

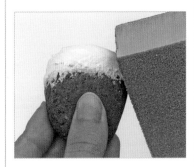

3 If you spot any bumpy surfaces on your new pebbles, use some sandpaper to lightly sand the bumpy areas. This commonly happens in the area where the filler and the rock meet. This will help to make the pebble and filler one whole shape.

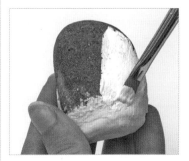

4 Finally, apply white acrylic paint all over your new shapes. You can now design and paint your altered pebbles!

FINISHING TOUCHES

Once you've finished your painted rocks, there are a number of things you can do with them. You might just varnish them to give them a bit of shine and protection – or you might want to try drilling holes in them to turn them into pendants.

YOU WILL NEED

- ☑ Goggles
- ☑ Small, smooth, flat pebbles
- ☑ Piece of wood
- ☑ Rotary tool
- ☑ Diamond core drill bit (2.25 x 4.2 mm)
- ☑ Dremel collet nut (the same diameter)
- ☑ Eucerin hand lotion
- ☑ Paper towel

DRILLING HOLES IN PEBBLES

Drilling pebbles allows you to create pendants, which can be attached to a chain or string. Please note that you can buy pebbles predrilled so if this isn't for you, don't let the thought of drilling put you off the idea altogether.

Paint your pendant in your favourite design, whether animals, patterns or colour! To start producing pendants, however, you need a special rotary tool, such as the Dremel 4000. Before you attempt this, make sure that you have fully read the manufacturer's instructions and taken all safety precautions recommended.

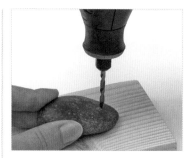

1 Put on your goggles. Firmly hold your stone on top of the piece of wood, with your left hand (if you are right-handed).

VARNISHING THE PEBBLE

Just one layer of varnish will make the colours of your pebble stand out. It also protects the pebble and keeps the paint from peeling off. There is a choice of two types: matt or gloss varnish. Both have the same protective properties but vary in their final effect: gloss varnish will make your pebble look shiny so opt for matt varnish if you want to avoid this.

Varnish comes in liquid or spray form. A spray varnish will make it easier and quicker to cover all sides of the pebble. If using liquid varnish, you need to use a large paintbrush for an even coverage. It is important to wash your brush after varnishing.

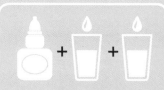

MAKING VARNISH

Did you know that you can make your own varnish? Mix together one part PVA glue with two parts water and simply apply to your pebble!

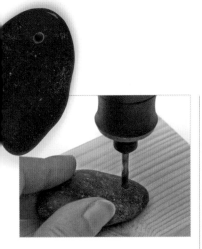

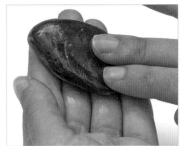

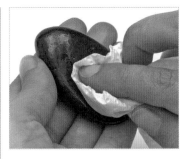

2 Turn on the rotary tool with your free hand and hold it so it is perpendicular to the pebble. Slowly begin drilling. Let the weight of the tool do the work for you. You'll feel when it breaks through to the wood. With small beach pebbles, drilling usually takes about 2–3 minutes.

3 Rub unscented Eucerin lotion into the pebble. This helps to condition the stones so that the natural oils from your skin won't leave uneven dark spots. It also enriches the natural colour of the stone so it isn't dusty looking from the drilling.

4 Allow the lotion to absorb into the stone for a few minutes, then wipe off any excess lotion with a clean, dry paper towel.

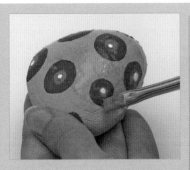

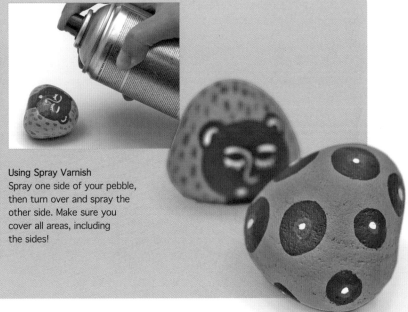

Using Liquid Varnish
When your pebble is complete and the paint is dry, you can apply varnish to one side of your pebble. Allow to dry for a few minutes (a hair dryer is useful here) and then turn your pebble over and varnish the other side.

Using Spray Varnish
Spray one side of your pebble, then turn over and spray the other side. Make sure you cover all areas, including the sides!

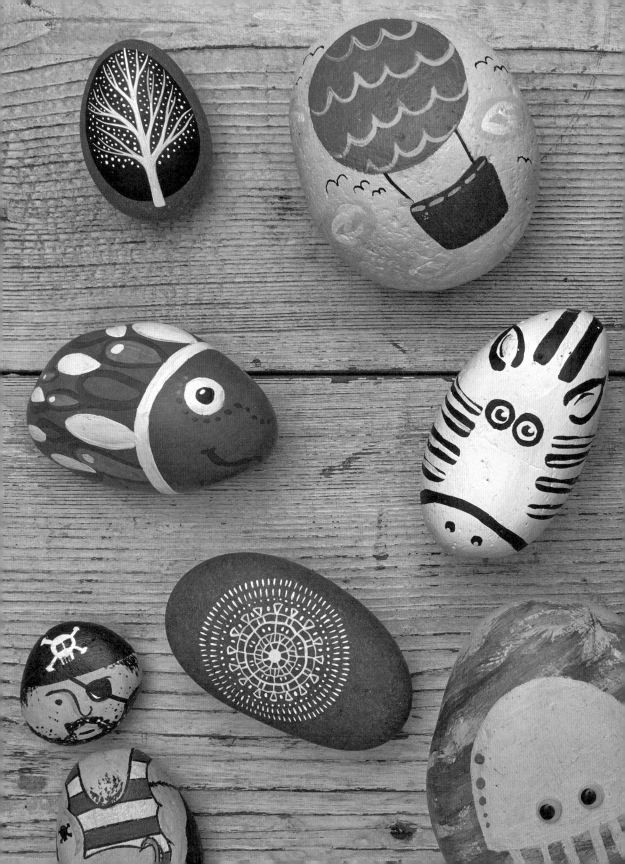

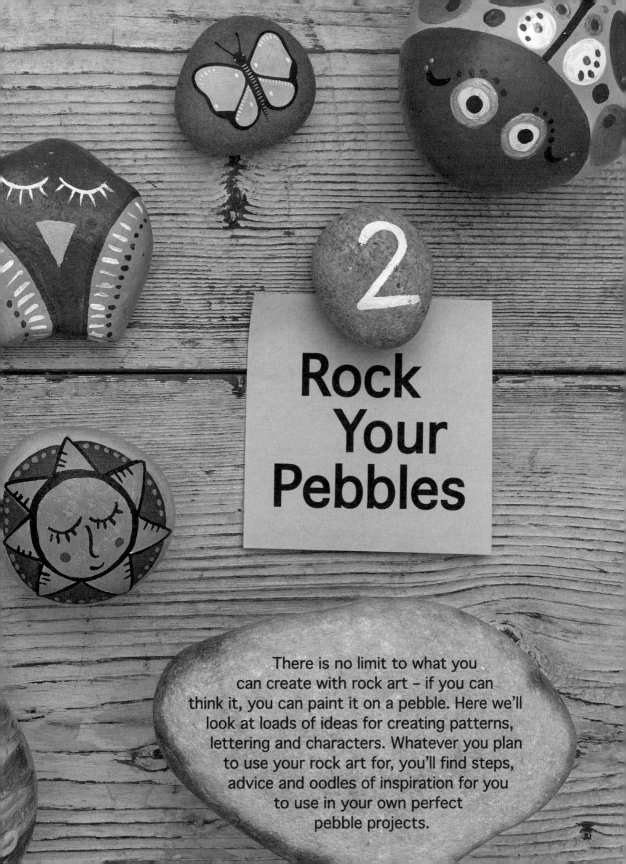

2
Rock Your Pebbles

There is no limit to what you can create with rock art – if you can think it, you can paint it on a pebble. Here we'll look at loads of ideas for creating patterns, lettering and characters. Whatever you plan to use your rock art for, you'll find steps, advice and oodles of inspiration for you to use in your own perfect pebble projects.

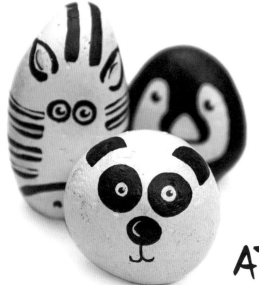

AT THE ZOO

There are thousands of cute animal characters to choose from and they make really fun rock art projects. This project looks solely at black and white animals, which are surprisingly easy to create and are instantly recognisable. But with a few more colours of paint, you can create almost any animal face.

YOU WILL NEED

☑ Round pebble
☑ Damp cloth
☑ White and black craft paint
☑ Paintbrushes
☑ Pencil
☑ Black marker pen (optional)
☑ Varnish

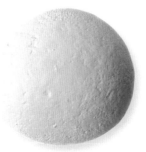

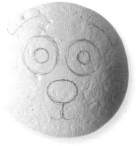

1 Choose a smooth, round pebble and clean it with a damp cloth. Paint it with white paint, applying a second layer if necessary. Paint one side and let it dry before turning over and painting the reverse. Let it dry.

2 Using a pencil, draw the basic features of a panda. This is simpler than you'd think: a pair of round eyes, an oval-shaped nose towards the centre and a simple linear mouth shape. Add a pair of ears above the eyes.

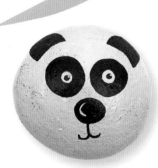

3 Fill in the facial features in black paint or marker pen. Make sure the pencil does not show anymore. Gently use an eraser if necessary.

4 Using the white paint again, add a blob of paint in each eye and, when dry, add a tiny dot of black inside this. Add a little highlight in the centre of each eye, as shown. This will bring your panda's face to life. Add a 'c' shape inside the nose. Allow it to dry and then add a layer of varnish.

VARIATIONS Try these black-and-white beasties

Penny the Penguin >

Although this cutie is more black than white, you should still start by painting your pebble white all over. It is much easier to add the black details over the top than the other way around. Use a marker pen for the fiddly bits.

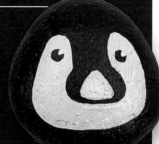

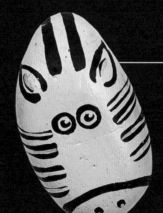

< Stripes the Zebra

Choose an elongated pebble for a zebra to match the length of his face. Simply add black stripes on the sides and top of the head, along with a pair of eyes, ears and dotted nostrils: instant zebra!

Carmen the Cow >

Use an oval-shaped pebble to design your own cow. Carmen has two black patches, one of which goes over her left eye. Add a pair of horns next to the ears, and nostrils towards the bottom of the pebble.

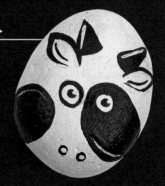

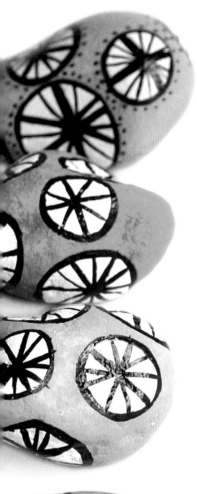

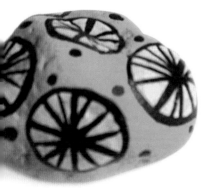

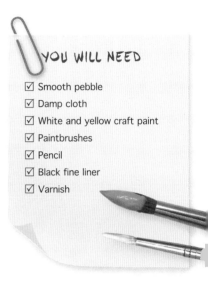
BICYCLE WHEELS

This simple motif, which resembles a bicycle wheel and its spokes, is a great way to start experimenting with patterned pebbles. Use a thick black outline and bright colours to create eye-catching abstract pebbles to decorate your home – the more you have, the better.

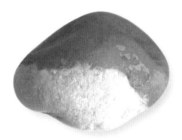

1 Choose a smooth pebble and clean it with a damp cloth. Paint the whole pebble in yellow – paint one side, wait for it to dry and then turn over to paint the reverse.

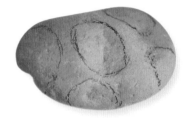

2 With a pencil, draw different-sized circles all over your pebble, front and back.

VARIATIONS   Add these variations to your design wheelhouse

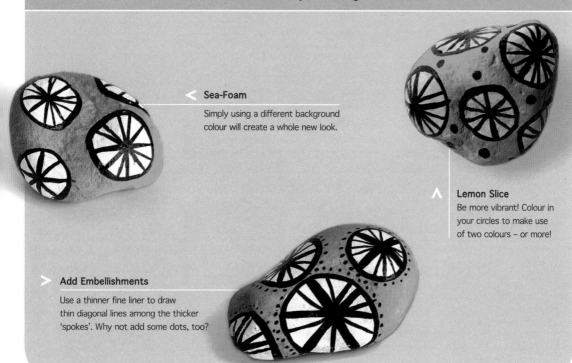

Sea-Foam

Simply using a different background colour will create a whole new look.

Lemon Slice

Be more vibrant! Colour in your circles to make use of two colours – or more!

Add Embellishments

Use a thinner fine liner to draw thin diagonal lines among the thicker 'spokes'. Why not add some dots, too?

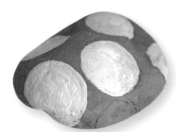

3 Paint the insides of your sketched circles in white paint. Apply a second layer if you find it is not white enough. Let the paint dry.

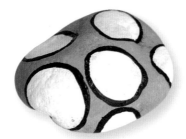

4 Using the black fine liner, draw bold outlines around each of the painted white circles.

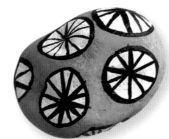

5 Draw five or more straight lines in the circle, all intersecting at the middle point, to create a wheel effect. Once dry, varnish the whole pebble.

UNDER THE SEA

Observe the shades, forms, colours and fresh smells of the sea and channel all this onto pebbles with ocean-inspired abstracts. These would look great with any of the ideas on pages 48–49, 66–67 and 96–97. Why not give your goldfish a tank fit for Triton?

YOU WILL NEED

- ☑ Large pebble
- ☑ Damp cloth
- ☑ Four shades of blue craft paint
- ☑ Paintbrushes
- ☑ Chalk
- ☑ White craft paint or marker pen
- ☑ Varnish

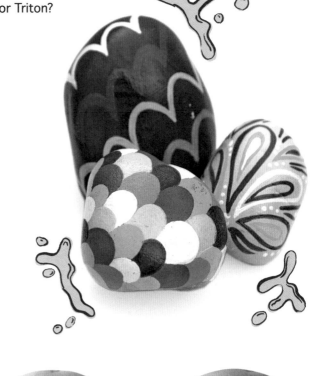

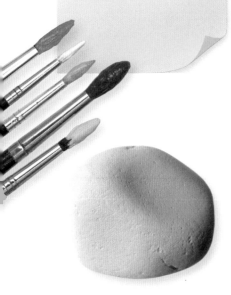

1 Clean your chosen pebble with a damp cloth and then paint it all over with your lightest blue paint. Paint one side and let it dry before turning it over to paint the reverse.

2 Once the paint is dry, use chalk to sketch four spiralled waves merging into each other in whatever design you like. Imagine the waves of the sea while you are creating this pattern.

3 Paint two waves in the lighter two of the three remaining blue paints and allow to dry.

VARIATIONS Make a splash with these other watery designs

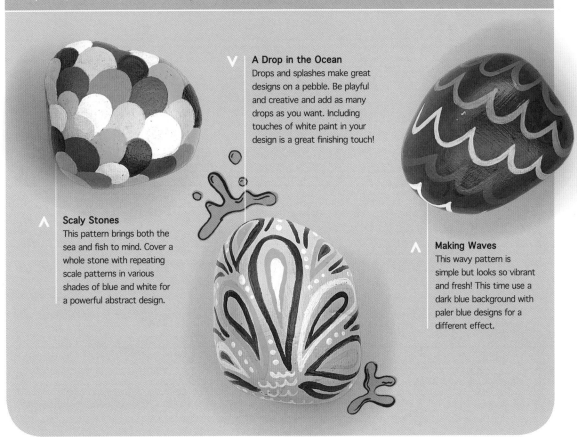

A Drop in the Ocean
Drops and splashes make great designs on a pebble. Be playful and creative and add as many drops as you want. Including touches of white paint in your design is a great finishing touch!

Scaly Stones
This pattern brings both the sea and fish to mind. Cover a whole stone with repeating scale patterns in various shades of blue and white for a powerful abstract design.

Making Waves
This wavy pattern is simple but looks so vibrant and fresh! This time use a dark blue background with paler blue designs for a different effect.

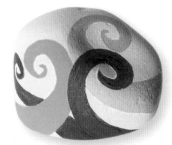

4 When dry, paint the last two waves with the darkest blue paint.

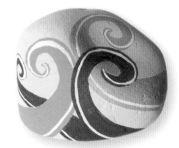

5 With your white paint or pen, outline your waves to create a fresher look.

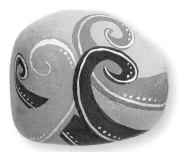

6 Add a couple of dots around the top and bottom parts of each of the waves. Allow to dry and then add a layer of varnish all over the pebble.

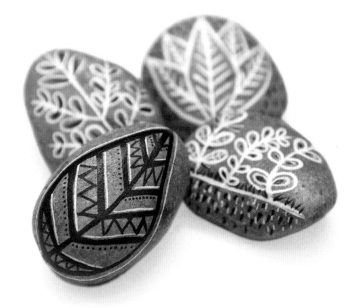

YOU WILL NEED

- ☑ Round pebble
- ☑ Damp cloth
- ☑ White chalk
- ☑ White and black craft paint or marker pens
- ☑ Paintbrushes
- ☑ Varnish

ROCK GARDEN

Nature-inspired designs work fantastically well on pebbles and will look beautiful adorning your garden or your home. These ideas show how to create really impactful designs using just black and white, but check out pages 58–59 and 64–65 for ideas about how to use colour in this subject.

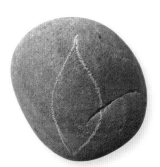

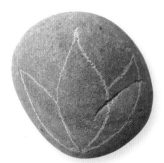

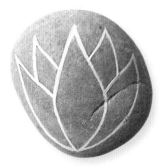

1 Choose a smooth, round pebble and clean it with a damp cloth. Use white chalk to draw a single leaf shape in the centre of the pebble.

2 Add a similar shape on each side of the central leaf, this time tilted at an angle.

3 Add two more smaller leaves in the gaps and outline all five leaves in white paint or marker pen. Gently rub off any chalk that is still showing.

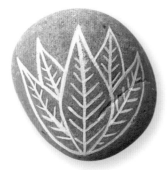

4 Draw a vertical line going down the centre of each leaf.

5 Still using white, add several short lines branching out from each vertical line for each leaf; these will be the leaf veins.

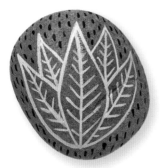

6 Finally, to make your design really stand out, add short black lines to the background area. Allow to dry and then add a layer of varnish.

VARIATIONS Not your garden-variety rocks

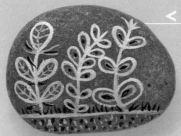

< Botanical Boulder

Why not draw two or three (or more!) plants on the same pebble and create a simple garden scene? This would be great for a really large, long pebble decorated with a whole row of plants.

> Branch Out

Draw five branches and add small leaves along each branch to create this dainty plant. Add more branches if you want to! Check out pages 36–37 for more treelike designs.

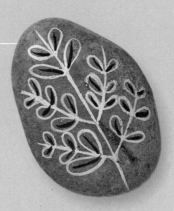

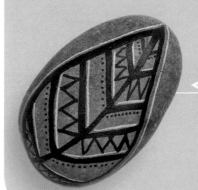

< Abstract Additions

Go wild and decorate a big leaf with abstract designs. Play around with black and white patterns, and add dots, lines and zigzags. The bold black lines make a brilliant effect.

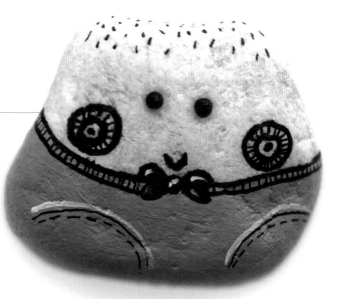

> The Chubby One

The perfect pebble for this face would be a big round one. Feel free to add parts of the body if the pebble shape allows this. You can draw part of a T-shirt or trousers, such as the big blue jeans that this chubby guy is wearing. You can partially use the texture and colour of the pebble and paint the rest in colour.

< The Cutie

Get inspired by someone who is cute looking or maybe by your favourite cartoon character. Here is a cute monster with a mauve face and red hair. Make sure to add cute features such as big, round eyes and a small, sweet smile.

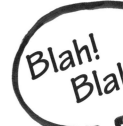

> The Big Mouth

Instead of painting the whole pebble, you can make use of the pebble's natural texture and colour. This is a very fast way of painting any design since you don't need to wait for any paint to dry. Use a black marker or black paint with a thin paintbrush to make the outline of the big mouth's features!

FUNNY FACES

Pebbles are the perfect shape for heads and faces. You can find a selection of head shapes – elongated, chubby, squarish, round! Explore different types of faces by applying features that you think best suit the pebble shape.

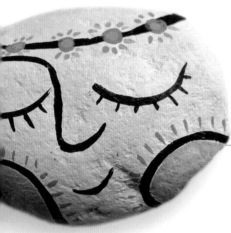

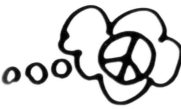

< The Hippie

Design a peaceful-looking face depicting love and serenity. Add a small crown of flowers around the head using colourful paint. Draw the face in any colour you like!

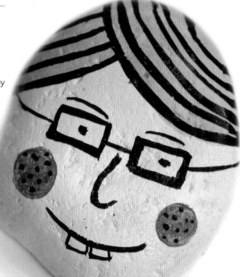

> The Geek

Make this face look stereotypically nerdy by adding freckles, big front teeth and thick glasses. Paint the face with flesh-coloured paint and add details with black paint or marker.

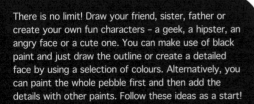

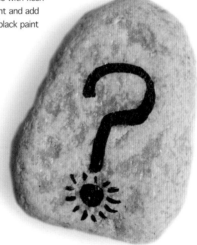

There is no limit! Draw your friend, sister, father or create your own fun characters – a geek, a hipster, an angry face or a cute one. You can make use of black paint and just draw the outline or create a detailed face by using a selection of colours. Alternatively, you can paint the whole pebble first and then add the details with other paints. Follow these ideas as a start!

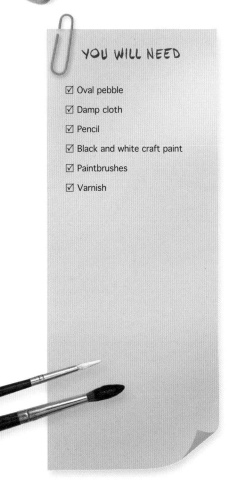

YOU WILL NEED

- ☑ Oval pebble
- ☑ Damp cloth
- ☑ Pencil
- ☑ Black and white craft paint
- ☑ Paintbrushes
- ☑ Varnish

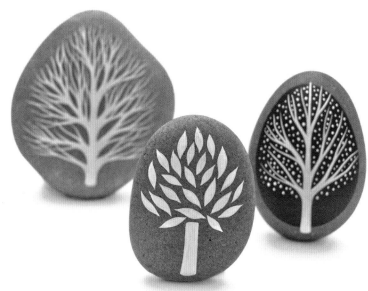

INTO THE WOODS

These intricate tree designs are a great way to practise your fine brush work, although you could use a fine liner or marker pen to make things easier for yourself. Combined with the black and white leaves on pages 32–33, a few of these would look stunning in a 3D frame (see page 109).

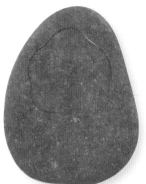

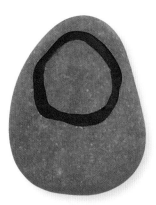

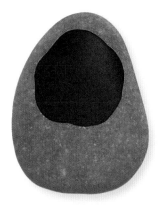

1 Choose a smooth, oval pebble and clean it with a damp cloth. Draw a wavy circle in pencil. This will be the top part of your tree.

2 Using black paint, carefully follow the line you've drawn in pencil.

3 Fill in the middle of the shape, making sure the black paint covers evenly. Apply a second layer of paint if necessary. Allow it to dry.

VARIATIONS Why not branch out and try these designs?

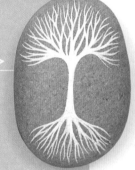

Lots of Leaves >

For a striking, simple design, paint many little leaf shapes in a rough circle and then add a simple trunk beneath them. Take the time to create precise, clean edges for maximum effect.

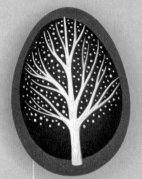

Great Oaks

This design is wonderful for a larger stone. With a fine paintbrush, start with the trunk and then gradually add the branches, working from top to bottom. Patience is required, but the result is worth it!

∧ Winter Scene

This eye-catching design was created by painting an oval shape with black paint; once dry add finely painted tree branches and a trunk in white. Finish with tiny spots for the leaves.

Put Down Roots >

For an interesting variation, paint a tree with roots. An oval-shaped or longer stone is perfect for this design. Remember to leave space underneath the trunk.

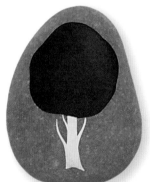

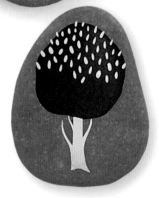

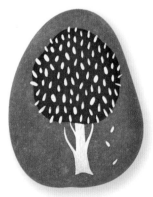

4 Using a fine paintbrush and some white paint, create a simple trunk for your tree.

5 Using the same fine brush, paint a series of small dashes to represent leaves, working from the top of your tree downwards to avoid smudging the wet paint.

6 Finish the leaves on the tree and also add a couple of falling leaves. Let it dry and then apply a coat of varnish to finish.

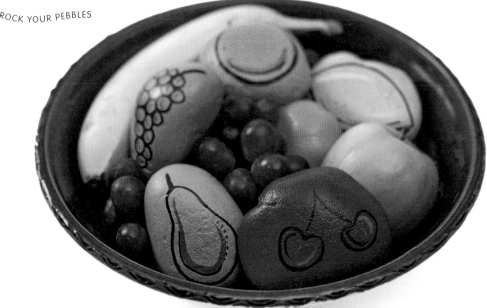

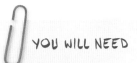
☑ Lemon-shaped pebble

☑ Damp cloth

☑ Yellow, black and white craft paint

☑ Paintbrushes

☑ Chalk

☑ Black marker pen (optional)

☑ Varnish

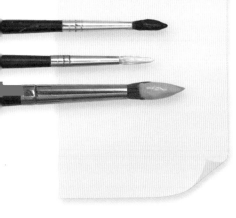

FRUIT SALAD

The fruity designs on this page cleverly combine colour and the shape of the pebble with a simple graphic line drawing to create really quick and simple but perfect pieces of fruit. A few of these in a fruit bowl would look really fun.

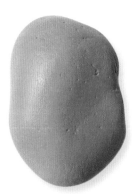

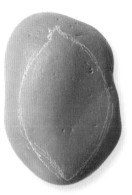

1 Select a pebble that most closely resembles a lemon shape and clean it with a damp cloth. Paint it all over with yellow paint, adding a second layer if necessary.

2 Once the paint is dry, use the chalk to sketch the basic shape of a lemon, using most of the space on your yellow pebble.

VARIATIONS   Pick your favourite!

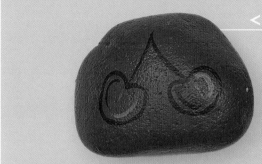

The Cherry on Top

A wide pebble would suit a pair of cherries. Use a lighter pink for highlights to create a shadowy effect on both cherries.

A Lovely Bunch >

This pebble is the perfect shape for a bunch of grapes. Draw plenty of circles close to each other, add a stem, and your rock is instantly transformed.

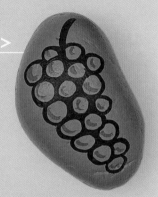

< Pear-Shaped

To draw the perfect pear, simply paint a lightbulb shape and finish it off by adding a small black stem right at the top.

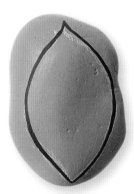

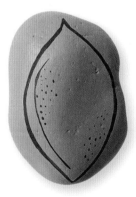

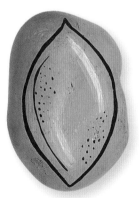

3 Go over the sketch with black paint or marker pen, using a bold, graphic line.

4 Next, add a thin, curved line inside the left side of the lemon. Add some black spots around your pebble.

5 Using white or light yellow paint, add some highlights to the lemon. Allow to dry completely and then add a layer of varnish.

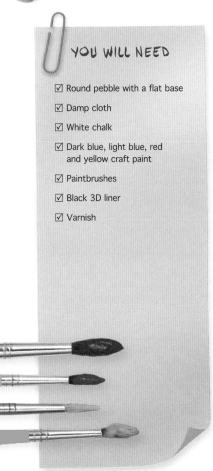

YOU WILL NEED

- ☑ Round pebble with a flat base
- ☑ Damp cloth
- ☑ White chalk
- ☑ Dark blue, light blue, red and yellow craft paint
- ☑ Paintbrushes
- ☑ Black 3D liner
- ☑ Varnish

WISE OWLS

Select a stone with a flat, even base and create characters that stand up on their own, like these fun, quirky owls. Remember that the back will be visible, too, so don't forget those tail feathers.

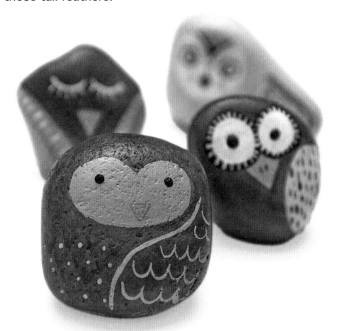

VARIATIONS How about these feathered friends?

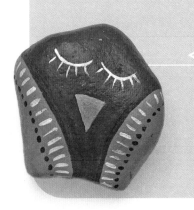

< Lady Owlina

Shy and sophisticated, she stands up too! Make use of different-shaped standing pebbles in creative ways – don't forget to use the back as well.

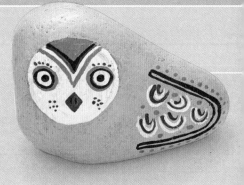

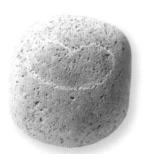

1 Choose a pebble with a flat base that will stand upright, and clean with a damp cloth. Use white chalk to outline the shape of the owl's head.

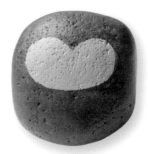

2 Paint the inside of the owl's head with light blue paint and the rest of the pebble with dark blue paint.

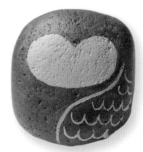

3 Paint the outline of the right wing in light blue and add small feathery patterns along it.

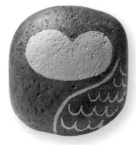

4 Next add some body markings next to the wing with red paint.

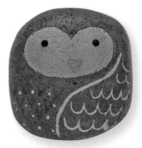

5 Using your 3D liner, add small black blobs for the eyes. Add a beak using yellow paint. You can also put some yellow spots on his body feathers.

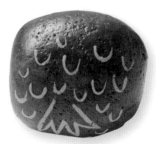

6 Add some light blue feathers on the back of the pebble and a tail at the bottom. Once dry, varnish all over.

WHOOO! WHOOO!

< **Folky Owl**

Let the shape of your pebble inspire your style of owls and other creatures. The shape of this pebble really suits this Russian doll-inspired owl.

Wise Old Owl >

This owl looks like he can say a few wise words. Notice how the black and white lines around his eyes make them look bigger and wiser!

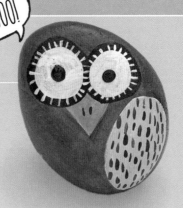

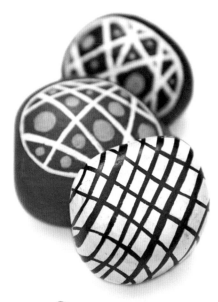

LET'S GET LINEAR

Make use of straight lines to create remarkable patterns, and see how these patterns can be applied to any shaped pebble of yours. Paint parallel lines or intersecting ones along your pebble. Find out which is your style!

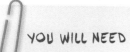

YOU WILL NEED

- ☑ Round pebble
- ☑ Damp cloth
- ☑ Black, white and yellow craft paint
- ☑ Paintbrushes
- ☑ White chalk
- ☑ Varnish

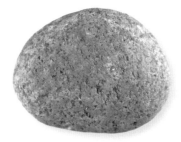

1 Choose a smooth, round pebble, and clean it with a damp cloth.

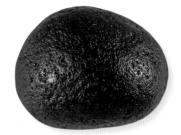

2 Paint your pebble all over in black. Cover the whole pebble – you may want to paint one side first, let it dry and then paint the other side.

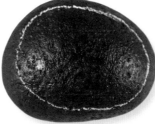

3 Using the chalk, create a circular shape on the front of your pebble.

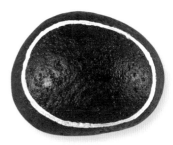

4 Using a thin paintbrush, go over the chalked line with white paint.

VARIATIONS Try out these straight-line styles!

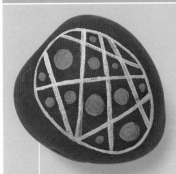

Rosy Red
Try replacing the black background with red for a totally different, eye-popping look.

Stay Natural
Show off the natural colour of the stone by painting only the middle part. Play around with different colours and add some finishing touches to the circular line.

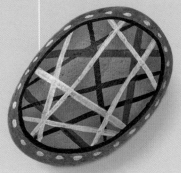

Black and White Basketweave
Go around your pebble, crossing lines from the back to the front. Black and white gives an elegant effect, but experiment with different colours.

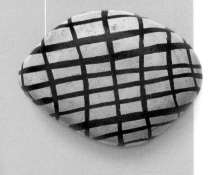

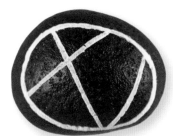

5 Still using the white paint, paint a few straight lines intersecting each other within the boundaries of the circular shape.

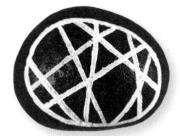

6 Keep crossing lines within the circular shape until you are happy that the design is well balanced.

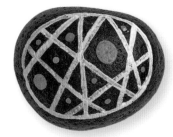

7 Add dots of varying sizes in yellow paint between the crossed lines. Once completely dry, add a layer of varnish all over.

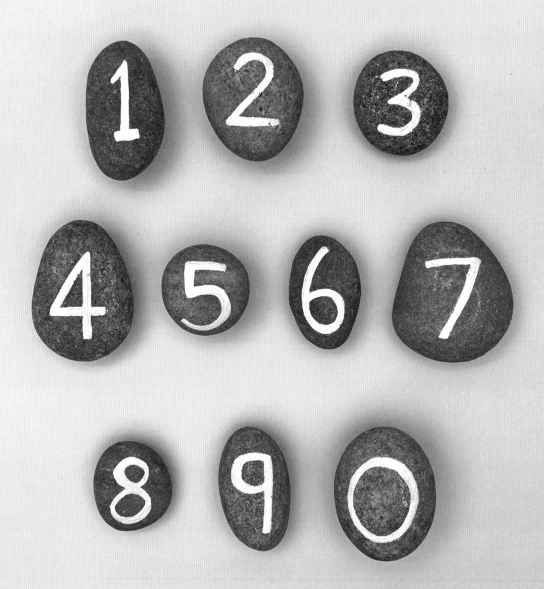

EASY AS ABC

Pebbles painted with letters and numbers can be used in so many great ways. From unique place names (see pages 112–113), to names spelled out on bedroom doors, or a way to make maths and spelling fun for your child, use these pebbles as a guide or play around with your own individual typography style.

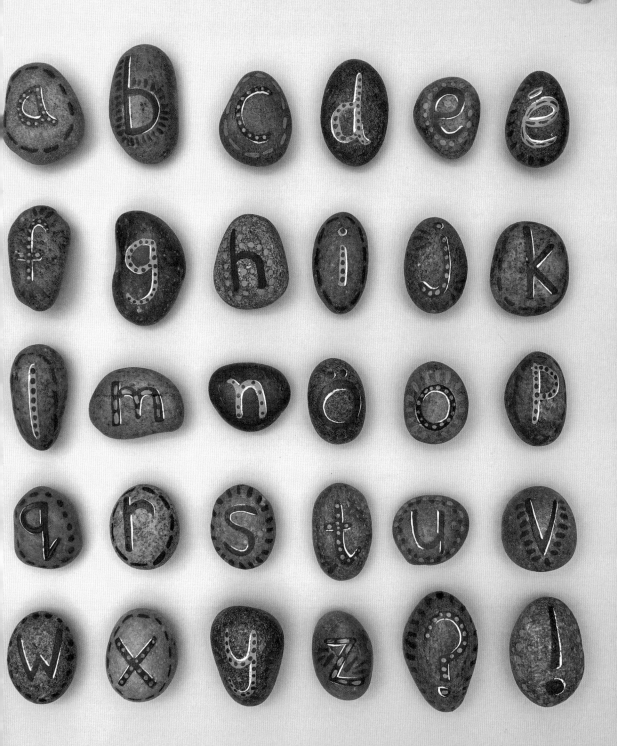

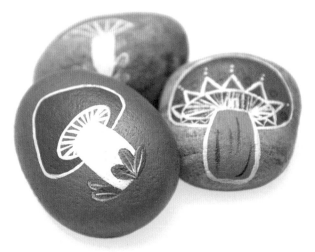

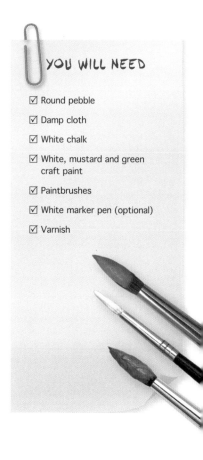

MUSHROOMS

Mushrooms are great fun to paint because they come in so many different shapes, sizes, designs and colours, and you can really let your imagination run wild. Why not create a pebble fairy ring at the bottom of your garden?

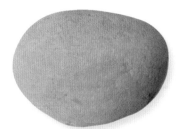

1 Choose a smooth, round pebble and clean it with a damp cloth.

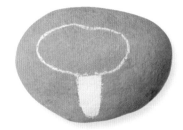

2 Use white chalk to draw a horizontal oval shape, which will be the head of the mushroom. Add the base of the mushroom slightly towards the side. Paint the base of the mushroom in white paint.

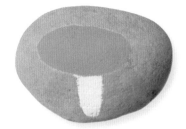

3 Next, paint the head of the mushroom in mustard paint.

VARIATIONS Try out these fun guys

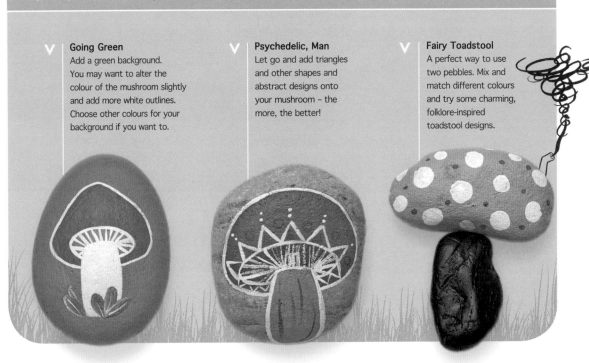

V Going Green
Add a green background.
You may want to alter the
colour of the mushroom slightly
and add more white outlines.
Choose other colours for your
background if you want to.

V Psychedelic, Man
Let go and add triangles
and other shapes and
abstract designs onto
your mushroom – the
more, the better!

V Fairy Toadstool
A perfect way to use
two pebbles. Mix and
match different colours
and try some charming,
folklore-inspired
toadstool designs.

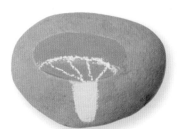

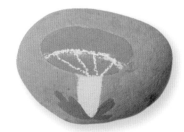

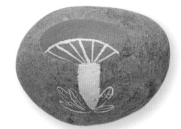

4 Using the chalk again, draw the 'gills' on the lower part of the mushroom head to represent the bottom of the head.

5 Add some leaves or grass in green paint next to the mushroom base.

6 Using a white marker pen or white paint and a fine paintbrush, go over the chalk lines on the mushroom head and add detail to the leaves. Allow to dry before adding a layer of varnish.

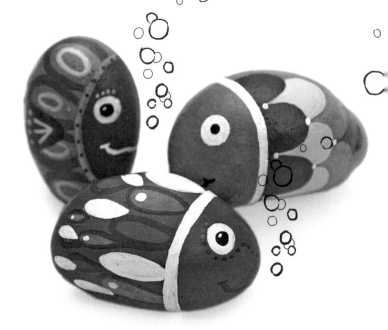

YOU WILL NEED

- ☑ Oval pebble
- ☑ Damp cloth
- ☑ Turquoise, dark blue, light blue, mustard and white craft paint
- ☑ Paintbrushes
- ☑ Chalk
- ☑ Black marker pen (optional)
- ☑ Varnish

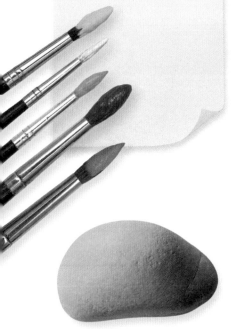

FISH OUT OF WATER

Fish are vibrant and full of interesting features and colours. Grab your paintbrush and pebble and make up your own new favourite fish! Mix and match with the ideas on pages 30–31, 66–67 and 96–97 to create a whole underwater scene.

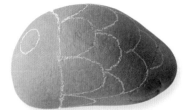

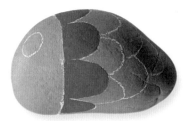

1 Choose a smooth, oval pebble and clean it with a damp cloth. Paint it all over with turquoise paint, applying a second layer if necessary. Paint one side, wait for it to dry and then turn the stone over to paint the reverse.

2 Using chalk, add a curved line at the 'front' of the pebble, leaving about two-thirds of the space for the scales. Add one eye and sketch out a four-row scale pattern. Add more rows if your pebble is bigger.

3 Start by painting the first row of scales in dark blue.

VARIATIONS These fellas will get you hook, line and sinker

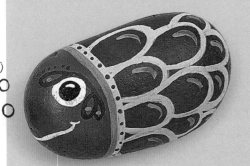

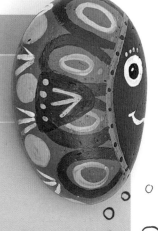

Flat Finn >

Fish come in all shapes and sizes. Use the pebble the other way around and create a tall fish like Finn here. Add a small fin along with the scales and patterns.

Tom Cruiser
You don't have to keep your decoration to the scales. Play around with your fish's eyes, too, and add spots and other decorative patterns.

Bubbles the Blowfish ∨
This fish looks particularly fancy with her different-coloured scales, and decorated eyes.

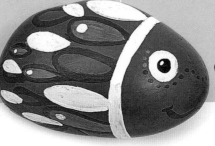

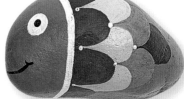

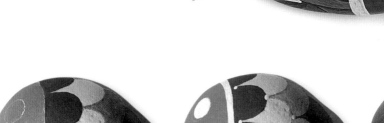

4 Now add light blue for the second row, mustard for the third row and finish off the last row with dark blue again.

5 In white paint, outline the section that divides the face from the scales and paint in the eye. Add extra detail with white dots on the scales.

6 Using black paint or a marker pen, add a black dot in the centre of the eye and a big smile to your fish. When completely dry, varnish to finish.

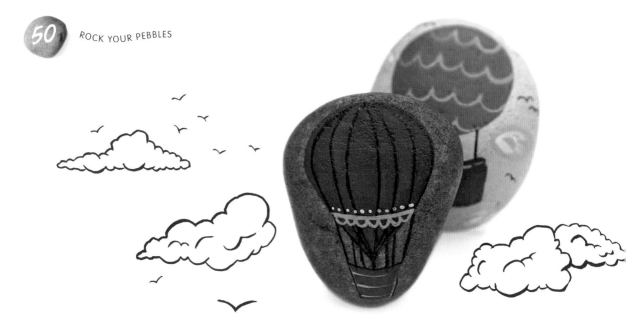

YOU WILL NEED

☑ Round, flat pebble

☑ Damp cloth

☑ Light blue, purple, dark red, black, turquoise, blue and white craft paint

☑ Paintbrushes

☑ Pencil

☑ Varnish

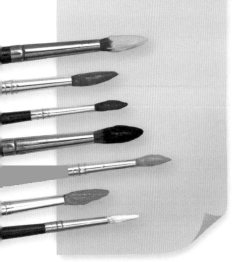

UP, UP AND AWAY!

From *Around the World in Eighty Days* to *The Wizard of Oz*, hot-air balloons are full of nostalgic charm and look beautiful painted on pebbles. Best of all, they're really easy to draw. Why not use one of these designs as your inspiration?

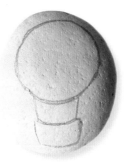

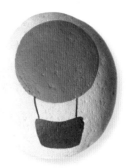

1 Choose a round, flat pebble and clean it with a damp cloth. Paint it all over with light blue paint. Paint one side and let it dry, then turn the pebble over to paint the reverse. Using a pencil, sketch a big circle in the top half of your pebble. At the bottom draw a rectangular shape for the wicker basket. Join the two shapes together with fine lines.

2 Next, paint the balloon in bright purple, the basket in dark red and go over the lines that join them together in black paint.

VARIATIONS Take your rock art sky high

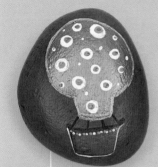

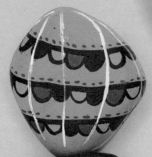

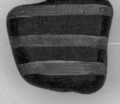

Vintage Balloon

This cute hot-air balloon has a vintage touch to it. Add more lines to bring the envelope and basket together.

Fit for a King

The great thing about hot-air balloons is that you can decorate them any way you want! Use gold paint and add spots to make your hot-air balloon look really special.

Rock the Basket

This fun 3D hot-air balloon consists of two pebbles. Make use of strange-looking squarish pebbles and use one for the basket!

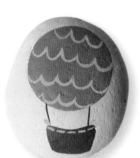

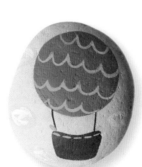

3 Decorate your hot-air balloon with turquoise paint, adding wavy patterns on the balloon shape and dotted lines on the basket.

4 Decorate the sky background with some clouds around your hot-air balloon, using blue and white paint.

5 Finally, add some birds flying through the clouds. Allow to dry before adding a layer of varnish.

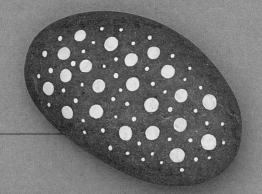

> **Go Dotty**

Cover a stone in spots! You can choose to vary the size of the spots, or even use several colours for different results.

< **As Simple as Stripes**

A steady hand is required for this, but it's still an easy design to paint! Vary the width of your stripes across the length of the stone, making some very fine while others are thicker.

> **Lots of Lovely Little Lines**

Taking a very tiny brush, paint rows of lines in varying sizes for a very simple but effective pattern.

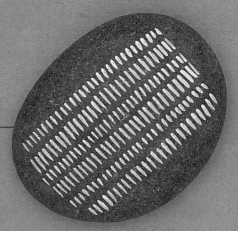

KEEP IT SIMPLE

If you are a minimalist, then you are probably on the right page! As fun as it is to come up with wacky designs, you can also create breathtaking designs using the simplest of repeating patterns. Keep the colours and shapes to a minimum and rely on your precision and steady hand to give your designs the 'wow' factor.

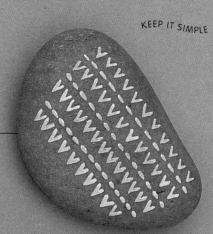

> Delicate Doodles

With a fine brush, paint small dashes
and triangular shapes in rows,
alternating between the two to create
a delicate pattern.

< Raindrops Keep Falling on My Head

Simple white raindrops make a beautiful
pattern when painted in rows – or you
could choose to place them randomly too.
You'll need a fine-tipped brush for these!

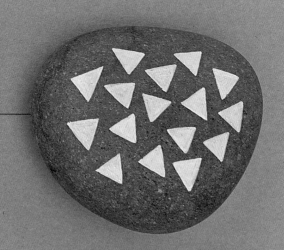

> Tiny Triangles

Triangles are a relatively easy shape to
paint and make a striking geometric
pattern. Vary the size of the triangles
for a slightly different look.

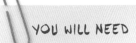

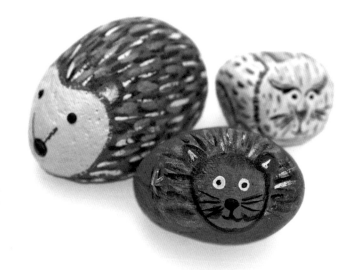

YOU WILL NEED

- ☑ Round pebble
- ☑ Damp cloth
- ☑ White chalk
- ☑ Light pink, brown, dark brown, white and mustard craft paint
- ☑ Paintbrushes
- ☑ Black 3D liner
- ☑ Varnish

PEBBLE PETS

The shape of pebbles allows many creatures and objects to come to life. You can create 3D animals by using all the sides of your pebbles and make your very own pebble pets.

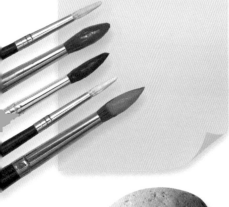

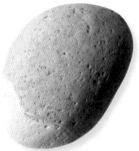

1 Choose a round pebble and clean it with a damp cloth. Start by sketching a face with chalk and then painting it in light pink.

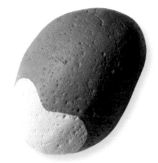

2 Select a light brown colour and use it to paint the whole body. This will provide the base under Harry Hedgehog's spikes.

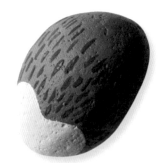

3 Using dark brown paint, paint short lines all over the body for the spikes. Don't worry too much about making them neat.

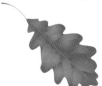

VARIATIONS Fall in love with these cuddly rocks

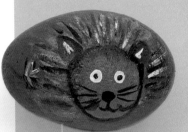

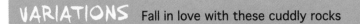

Hunny Bunny >

Rabbits can look great on pebbles. Use the whole top of the pebble to fit in her long ears, and remember to add a tiny, fluffy cottontail at the back.

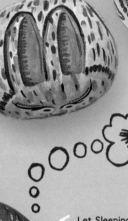

∧
Rory the Lion
Whether you make your lion fearsome or friendly like Rory, paint his mane in different shades of the same colour to add depth and shadow. Don't forget his tail.

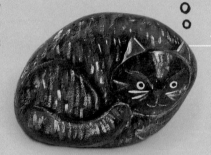

< **Let Sleeping Cats Lie**

Always let the pebble inspire you! This pebble had the perfect shape for a cosy kitty curled up by the fire. You can fit in the tail, legs and some paws, depending on the shape of your pebble.

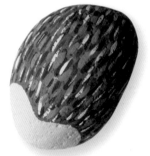

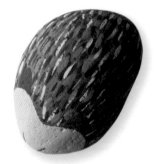

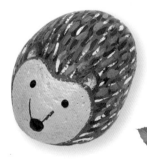

4 Next add some spikes in white and mustard paint. Don't worry if you cover some of the brown spikes, as the layering of different colours will give a sense of depth.

5 Add a pair of brown ears and then the shape of the nose using the same colour.

6 Use brown and white paint to add detail to the ears. Finally, use the 3D liner to add a big blob for the nose and two dots for the eyes. Allow to dry and then add a layer of varnish.

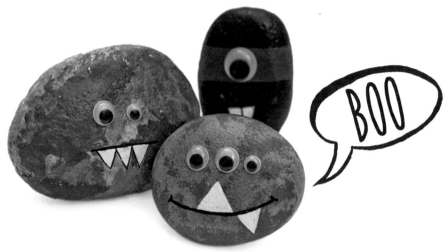

GOOGLY-EYED MONSTERS

YOU WILL NEED

- ☑ Pebble
- ☑ Damp cloth
- ☑ Turquoise, green and white craft paint
- ☑ Paintbrushes
- ☑ White chalk
- ☑ Black marker pen (optional)
- ☑ Varnish
- ☑ Googly eyes
- ☑ PVA glue (optional)

The best thing about making monster pebbles is that you can go for any form or shape, making them a great way to use odd-shaped pebbles you don't know what do to with. Give your monster some googly eyes – they can easily be applied to any surface and are perfect for giving your monster some personality.

VARIATIONS Try these bug-eyed brutes

Odious Owen >

You can utilise other materials to add embellishments, such as these felt ears. Play around with the teeth and eyes – it doesn't matter how many you give your monster!

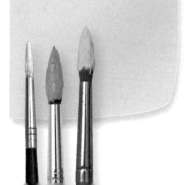

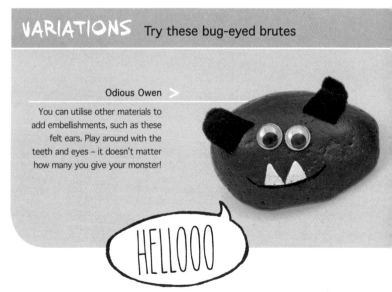

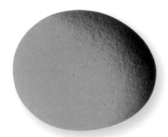

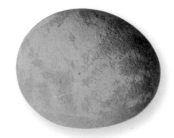

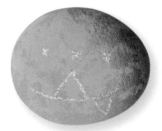

1 Clean your pebble with a damp cloth and then paint it all over with turquoise paint. Paint one side and leave to dry before turning over to paint the reverse. Apply a second layer if necessary.

2 Put a little green paint on your brush and then smudge the paint onto the pebble – anywhere you choose.

3 Use chalk to sketch a curved line for the mouth and then add an upwards and a downwards tooth. Place dots to mark the rough position of the eyes and help you to place the mouth.

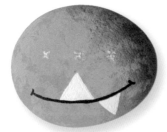

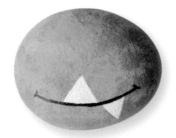

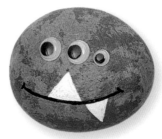

4 Fill in the teeth with white and when that is dry, go over the line for the mouth with a marker pen.

5 Allow to dry, gently rub off any visible chalk, and then apply a layer of varnish.

6 When the varnish has dried completely, stick three googly eyes onto your pebble, either using the self-adhesive backing on the eyes or with PVA glue.

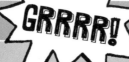

Diabolical Dave >

How about a monster with one big eye? Even these sharp white teeth can't make this smiley scamp look scary.

Fiendish Frank >

Make use of several bright colours and smudge them all over your pebble. This is a good one to try with larger pebbles. Eyes of different sizes will give a particularly monstrous look.

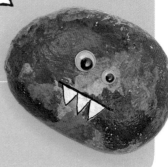

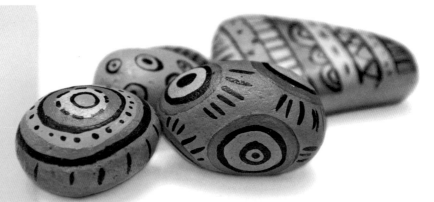

YOU WILL NEED

- ☑ Oval-shaped pebble
- ☑ Damp cloth
- ☑ White chalk
- ☑ Turquoise, red, yellow, black and blue craft paint
- ☑ Paintbrushes
- ☑ Varnish

COLOUR POPS

The designs on this page are inspired by pop art, with vibrant colours, simple shapes and bold, black outlines. If you are both an art and a colour lover, this will be one of your favourite designs. Find out how to get crazy and create some striking stones with some selected pop-art patterns!

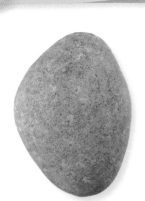

1 Select a smooth, oval-shaped pebble and clean with a damp cloth.

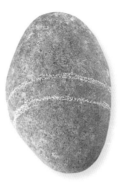

2 Using the chalk, draw two curved, parallel lines, forming a band around the pebble.

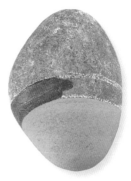

3 Paint the lower part of the pebble in turquoise and then the central band in red. Apply a second layer if the colours looks too light.

VARIATIONS Try these vibrant variations

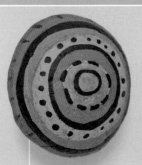

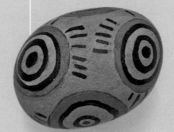

Ⅴ Hypno Pops
Concentric circles in bright primary colours and strong, black outlines will give you a hypnotic swirling spiral pattern.

Λ Colour Wheel
By drawing circles inside circles, you can design the perfect circular pop-art pattern. Make use of vibrant colours and don't forget to outline the shapes.

Λ Mexican Fiesta
Make use of a triangular pebble and create layers of triangles, semicircles, dots and stripes in bright colours to give your pebble a Mexican flavour.

OLÉ !

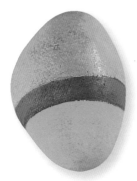

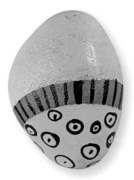

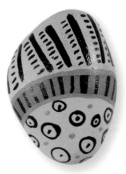

4 Next, paint the upper half of the pebble using yellow paint.

5 Once all the paint is completely dry, use black paint to create some round patterns on the turquoise part of the pebble and bold vertical lines along the red area.

6 Add longer and bolder black lines in the yellow area and add some dots along the lines. Using the blue paint, paint thin lines on either side of the red band. If you want, add some blue dots among the black circles. When dry, add a layer of varnish to finish.

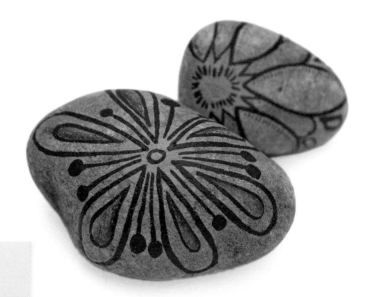

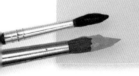

FLOWER POWER

These unique and stylised flowers will make truly beautiful decorative rocks. You only need two colours and a pencil to create these stunning graphic designs. Select your favourite flowers and colours, and express yourself.

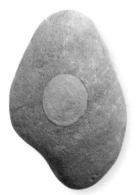

1 Choose a large grey pebble and clean it with a damp cloth. Paint a circle in the centre with violet paint.

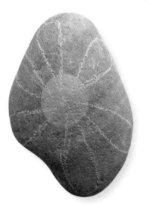

2 Once the paint is dry, use chalk to add a dot in the centre of the violet circle. Sketch petals starting from the centre dot, leaving a small space between each petal.

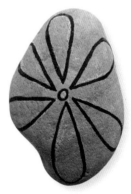

3 Outline the dot and the six petals with black paint or marker pen.

VARIATIONS Try some alternative floral delights

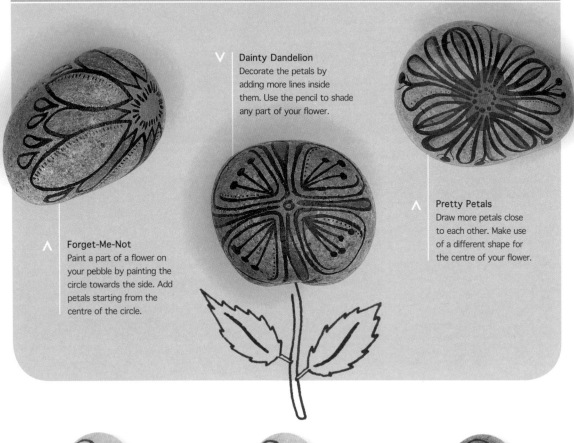

Dainty Dandelion
Decorate the petals by adding more lines inside them. Use the pencil to shade any part of your flower.

Forget-Me-Not
Paint a part of a flower on your pebble by painting the circle towards the side. Add petals starting from the centre of the circle.

Pretty Petals
Draw more petals close to each other. Make use of a different shape for the centre of your flower.

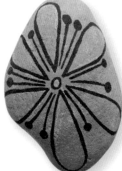

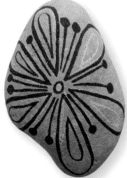

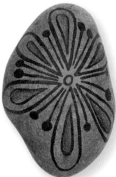

4 Add one or two long lines between each petal. Add a big dot at the end of each line.

5 Draw an inner petal inside all the existing petals with black paint or marker pen. Allow to dry.

6 Use your pencil to gently shade in the inner part of each petal. Finally, add a layer of varnish.

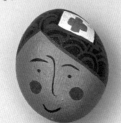
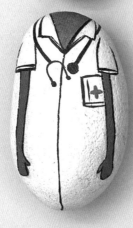
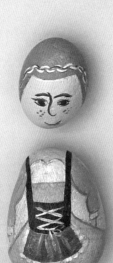
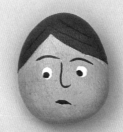
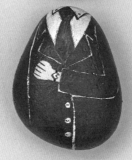
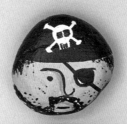
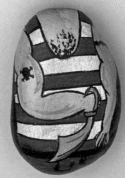
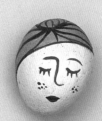
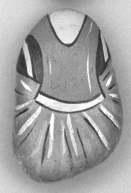
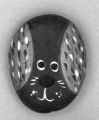
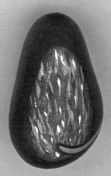

CONSEQUENCES

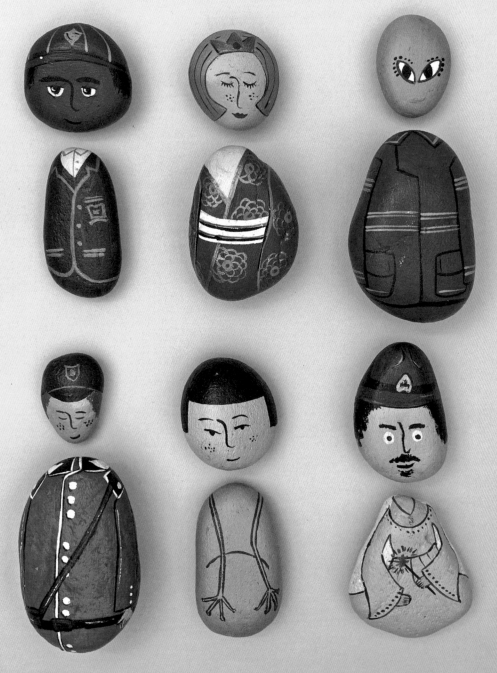

This is a super-fun way to create pebble people. Select a large, long pebble for the body and a smaller, rounder pebble for the head. Not only is this a nice way to make characters with lots of room to add in detailed costumes, but you can mix and match the heads and bodies with hilarious results!

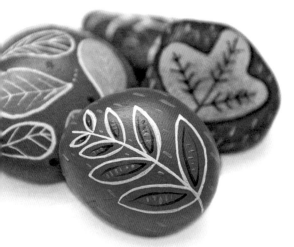

AUTUMN LEAVES

Create beautifully decorated pebbles to adorn your home or garden by taking your inspiration from nature. Stick with reds, yellows and browns and create classic autumn leaves. You can add creepy crawlies, or go abstract with bright colours and simple designs. For more muted, monochromatic leaves, check out the ideas on pages 32–33.

YOU WILL NEED

- ☑ Pebble
- ☑ Damp cloth
- ☑ Pencil
- ☑ Yellow, burgundy and black craft paint
- ☑ Black marker pen (optional)
- ☑ Paintbrushes
- ☑ Varnish

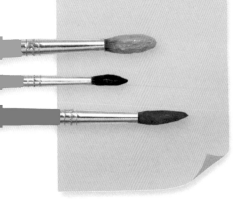

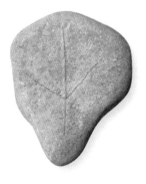

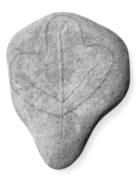

1 Choose a smooth pebble and clean it with a damp cloth. Use a pencil to draw branch-like lines in the centre of your pebble.

2 Next, draw a leaf shape around the branches, filling up most of your pebble.

VARIATIONS Give these leafy lovelies a try

Step into Spring >

Focus on a different season, and use green, purple, white and burgundy to create this pretty spring-inspired plant design. Here is your chance to come up with your own plant!

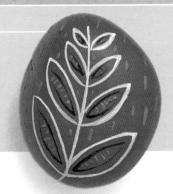

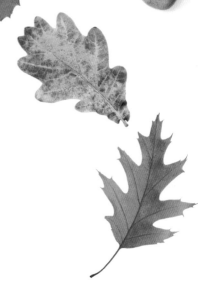

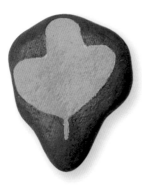

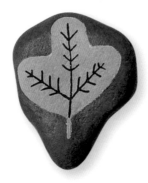

3 Paint the leaf shape yellow and the outer area burgundy.

4 Re-create the same branch-like lines, this time using black paint or marker pen. Add small lines along each branch.

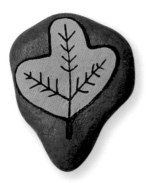

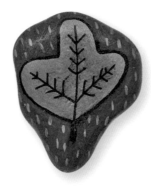

5 Now outline the whole yellow leaf with black paint or marker pen to make it stand out. Thicken the small stem at the bottom of the leaf.

6 To create an autumnal effect, add yellow lines or dots around your leaf. Allow to dry and then add a layer of varnish.

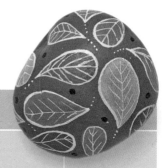

Bug Leaf >

Perfect for your little ones – paint a ladybird crawling on a simple green leaf. Why not experiment with other bugs too?

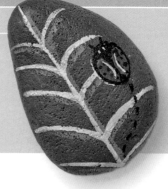

Falling Leaves

∧

Cover a round pebble in different-coloured leaves. Outline them in black or white to really make them stand out. Notice how many different colours you can use for leaves – the combinations are endless!

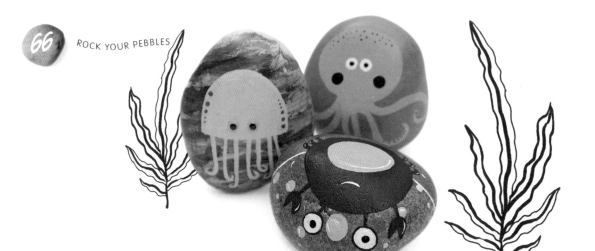

SUPER-CUTE SEA CREATURES

Why not make some adorable characters to add to an underwater scene? The trick is to focus on the basic shapes of your sea creature in a bold colour. Add bubbles and various shades of blue to bring your creatures to life. Try mixing and matching with the ideas on pages 30–31, 48–49 and 96–97 to create your own deep-sea scene.

YOU WILL NEED

- ☑ Oval pebble
- ☑ Damp cloth
- ☑ Pencil
- ☑ Turquoise, light purple and dark purple craft paint
- ☑ Paintbrushes
- ☑ Varnish
- ☑ Googly eyes
- ☑ PVA glue

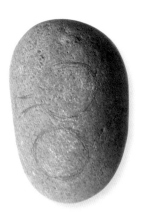

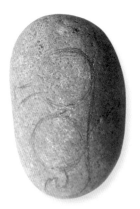

1 Choose an oval pebble and clean it with a damp cloth. Use a pencil to sketch out the basic shapes of a seahorse. Start by drawing two circles – one on the upper centre and one below it slightly to the left. Add a horn-shaped mouth.

2 Next, bring these shapes together by joining the head and belly and sketching a spiral tail towards the bottom of your pebble.

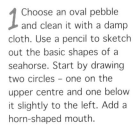

VARIATIONS   Add these guys to your marine menagerie

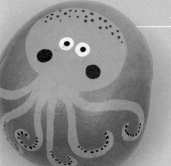

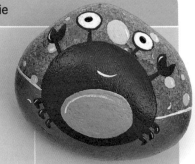

< In an Octopus's Garden

Remember to focus on the main forms of the creature – a big round head and lots of spiralled tentacles are all you need to instantly create a good-looking octopus! Add a pair of rosy cheeks and a few spots on its head.

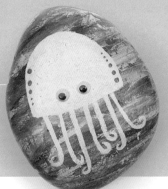

The Jolly Jelly >

Jellyfish are very easy and fun to draw. Start with a big semicircle and just add plenty of thin tentacles. Try painting the whole stone first in multiple shades of blue and adding white highlights to create a realistic backdrop.

Snap Happy

To re-create this happy crab, start by painting a big oval in the centre of the pebble. Add tiny feet on each side, claws and lastly the eyes sticking out of the top. You could paint on the eyes or add googly eyes for a different look.

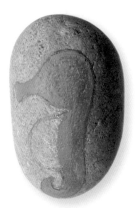

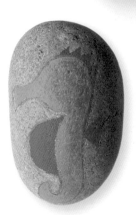

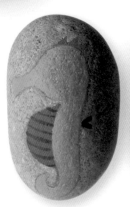

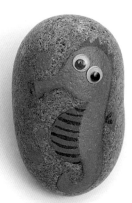

3 Fill in the whole body, except for the belly, with turquoise paint.

4 Using light purple paint, fill in the belly. Add a triangle for the dorsal fin and about three or four spikes over its head.

5 Add some stripes over the round belly and the fin with dark purple paint.

6 Paint on some bubbles around the seahorse and allow all the paint to dry before adding a layer of varnish. Finally, stick on a pair of googly eyes using PVA glue or the self-adhesive backing.

LIGHT AS A FEATHER

What's heavier – a ton of feathers or a ton of rocks? The juxtaposition of the weightless feather painted on a heavy stone makes this idea really fun. Feathers have a wonderful ethereal quality, and their defined and unique patterns make beautiful decorations for your home.

YOU WILL NEED

- ☑ Round pebble
- ☑ Damp cloth
- ☑ White chalk
- ☑ Yellow, white and dark blue craft paint
- ☑ Paintbrushes
- ☑ White marker pen (optional)
- ☑ Varnish

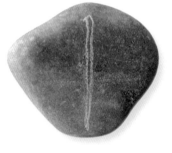

1 Choose a smooth, round pebble, and clean it with a damp cloth. Use white chalk to draw two vertical lines down the centre of your pebble. Join them together at both ends.

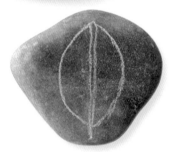

2 Draw curved lines on each side of your central line to create the outline of the feather.

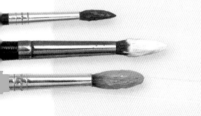

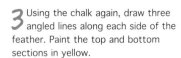

3 Using the chalk again, draw three angled lines along each side of the feather. Paint the top and bottom sections in yellow.

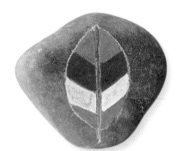

4 Fill in the other sections of the feather with white and dark blue paint.

VARIATIONS Try these heavyweight feathers

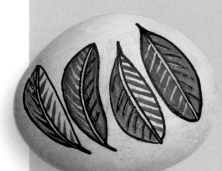

Fine Feather
Keep it simple and create a stylish, graphic feather using just two colours. Paint the lines as finely as you can.

Let the Feathers Fly
Choose a large pebble and decorate it with more than one feather. Play around with alternating colours and, if you are more adventurous, why not try shading the feathers too?

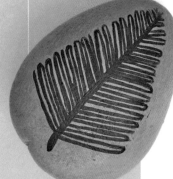

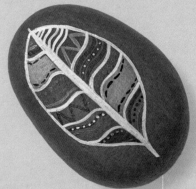

Aztec Feather
Create a highly detailed feather by adding extra sections and patterns and a bold background colour – there is no limit!

5 Outline the whole feather design using white marker pen or paint and fill in the thick line down the centre of the feather.

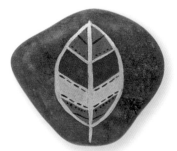

6 As a finishing touch, decorate the different sections with tiny lines and dots. Once dry, varnish your pebble all over for a gorgeous natural stone.

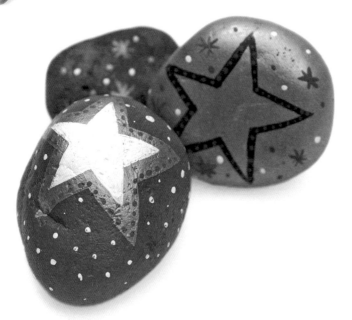

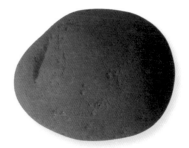

1 Choose a smooth, round pebble and clean it with a damp cloth. Paint it all over with dark pink paint. Paint one side and let it dry before painting the reverse.

ROCK STARS

Have you ever made a wish on the first star in the night sky? Paint your own lucky stars and let them shine on your pebbles! Gold or silver paint makes an excellent choice for star pebbles, but other colours will also look great.

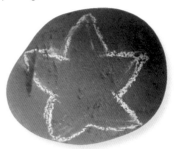

2 Use the chalk to sketch a star shape on your pebble, making use of all the space on the pebble's surface.

YOU WILL NEED

☑ Round pebble

☑ Damp cloth

☑ Dark pink, gold, white and purple craft paint

☑ Paintbrushes

☑ White chalk

☑ Varnish

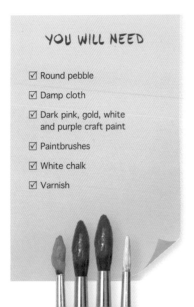

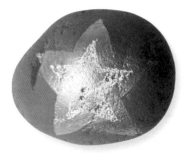

3 Paint the star in gold paint. Once dry, use the chalk again to sketch a smaller star inside the big golden star.

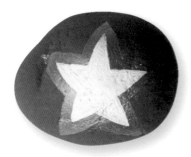

4 Paint the smaller inner star with white paint.

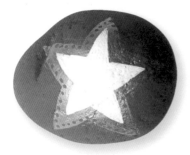

5 Add purple dots around the edge of the golden star.

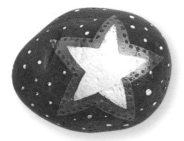

6 Add white dots around the star. Allow to dry completely and then add a layer of varnish to finish.

VARIATIONS Add a touch of stardust!

Star Light, Star Bright >

This design is so simple but so stylish! Use gold paint on a black background and cross several straight lines through a central point, just like an asterisk, for a big impact.

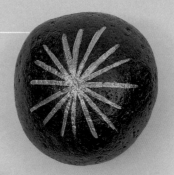

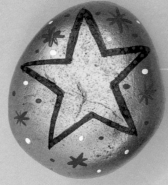

< Catch a Falling Star

To create this gold star pebble, choose a large rock. Paint a massive purple outline of a star on a golden background and then add smaller ones around it.

Starry Starry Night >

Why not fill your whole pebble with different types of stars using a variety of colours? A dark pebble will naturally create a galaxy effect!

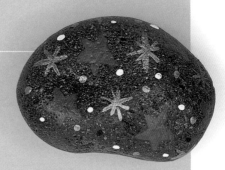

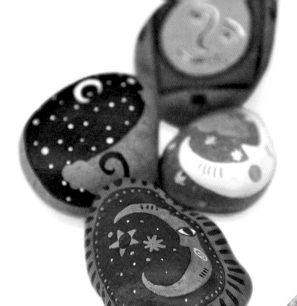

THE MAN IN THE MOON

Find out how to capture the moon in your rock art. Combine these with the ideas on pages 70–71 and 74–75 to create a celestial collection, or keep them as a symbolic token.

YOU WILL NEED

☑ Round pebble

☑ Damp cloth

☑ White chalk

☑ Turquoise, red, mustard, white and black craft paint

☑ Paintbrushes

☑ Black marker pen (optional)

☑ Varnish

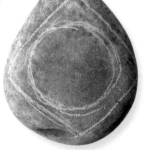

1 Choose a smooth, round pebble and clean it with a damp cloth. Use white chalk to draw a diamond shape in the centre of the pebble. Add a circle inside.

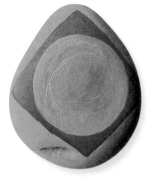

2 Paint the outer area in turquoise, the diamond in red and the circle in mustard.

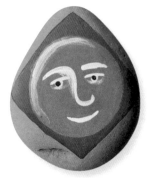

3 Using a thin paintbrush and white paint, add the eyes, nose and mouth to create the moon's face. Add two dots of black paint for the eyes.

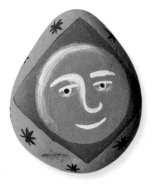

4 Paint black stars and mustard dots around the turquoise area.

VARIATIONS   You'll be over the moon with these

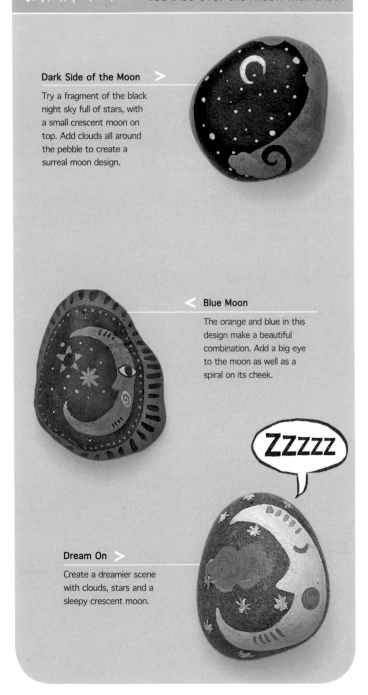

Dark Side of the Moon >

Try a fragment of the black night sky full of stars, with a small crescent moon on top. Add clouds all around the pebble to create a surreal moon design.

< **Blue Moon**

The orange and blue in this design make a beautiful combination. Add a big eye to the moon as well as a spiral on its cheek.

Dream On >

Create a dreamier scene with clouds, stars and a sleepy crescent moon.

ZZZZZ

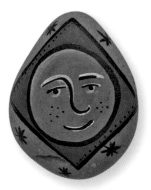

5 To make the design stand out, use black paint or a marker pen to outline the diamond shape. Add some freckles to the moon's face.

6 If you think the design looks a little flat, you can also outline the face features: simply go over them with black paint or marker. Allow to dry and then add a layer of varnish.

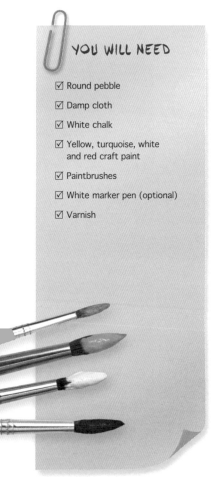

SUNNY SIDE UP

You can make your painted pebbles shine and emit happiness and light within your home or garden. Why not create a sun, a moon (pages 72–73) and some stars (pages 70–71) and display them all together.

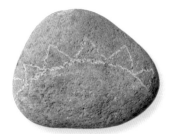

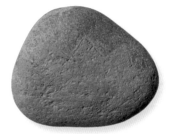

1 Choose a smooth, round pebble and clean it with a damp cloth. Use white chalk to create a semicircle across the centre of your pebble. Add the triangular rays of the sun along the curved line.

2 Paint the sun shape in yellow and the outer area in turquoise.

VARIATIONS Put a smile on your face with these sunny styles

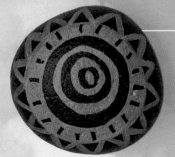

< A Ray of Sunshine

This large sun with lots of rays has an Aztec feel. If you like things more abstract, you could even play around with different colours – why not paint the sun blue if you want to?

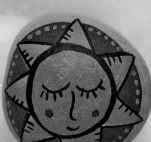

Here Comes the Sun >

Make your sun stand out and let it really shine by adding black outlines and eye-popping colours.

Sunshine on a Cloudy Day

This surreal design presents a sun within a bubble, surrounded by clouds. A perfect, dreamy summer's day.

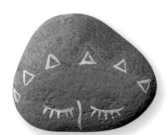

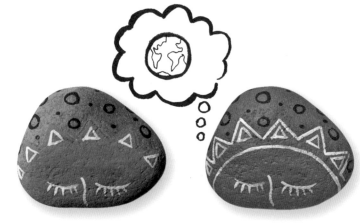

3 Using white paint or a white marker pen, add eyes and a nose to the sun. Then add white triangles to embellish the sun's rays.

4 Using red paint and a fine paintbrush, paint circles over the turquoise area.

5 Finally, add some white outlines to your design and allow to dry before varnishing.

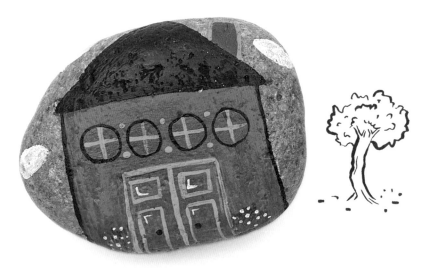

Home Sweet Home

These illustrated houses are quite realistic, but still pretty and colourful nonetheless. You can play around with roof styles, window shapes, doors, colours – it's up to you! Why not add some plants next to the main door or try to re-create your home in pebble form?

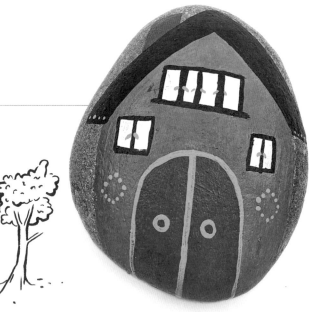

ROCKY ROAD

Be an architect and design your own house on a pebble! You can have lots of fun creating these, whether it's your dream house, your own house or the White House. Big pebbles are perfect for this fun architectural project – you could even make a whole village. These are ideal for both adults and kids.

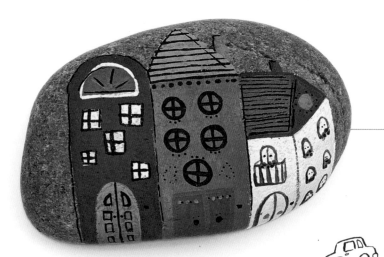

Street View

Using really large, flat pebbles allows more space for your houses. Design three or more next to each other, using different levels and widths. Vary the colours from house to house for a really vibrant effect. You could even try to re-create an iconic city skyline with familiar landmarks and architecture.

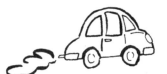

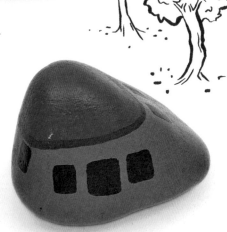

Bubble Houses

These are very simple, but their bubble effect makes them look very cute. Create a series of them and design a whole village. Play with them with your children or simply use them as a fun decoration for any windowsill, desk or shelf.

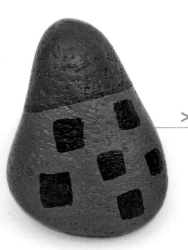

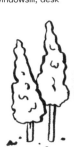

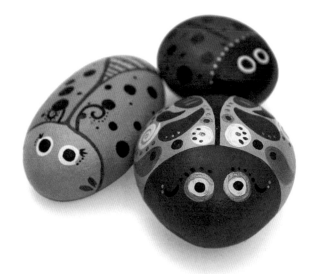

YOU WILL NEED

- ☑ Oval pebble
- ☑ Damp cloth
- ☑ Yellow, orange, white, red and black craft paint
- ☑ Paintbrushes
- ☑ White chalk
- ☑ Varnish

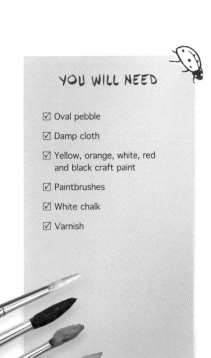

BRILLIANT BUGS

Bring your pebbles to life by painting colourful creepy crawlies on them. They are very simple to create as most of the space is taken up by the wings. Try to come up with your own crazy designs.

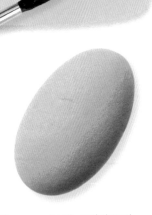

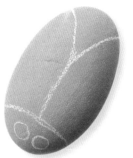

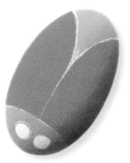

1 Choose a smooth, oval-shaped pebble and clean it with a damp cloth. Paint it with yellow paint on one side first and leave to dry before turning over to paint the reverse. Apply a second layer if necessary.

2 Use chalk to draw on the design. Start by drawing a vertical line right in the middle of the pebble. From there create the wings of the bug, by curving the line in diverging ways, towards the top of the pebble. Add a line for the head and two big bug eyes.

3 Paint inside the wings with orange paint and then paint the two round eyes with white paint.

VARIATIONS   Make your own marvellous minibeasts

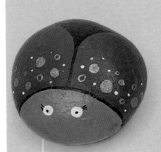

Beetle Mania
Double up and use both sides of the pebble to showcase two different designs. Draw a classic ladybird on one side, and on the other side, paint her with her wings out.

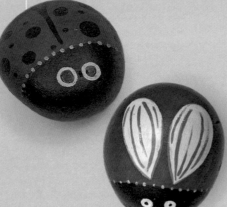

Pretty Pest
Use any shape or size of pebble and create chubby or dainty bugs. Play around with different colours and decorations to make your own species. The bug's wing is your canvas here!

Bohemian Beauty
Let your imagination go wild with wing decorations: add spirals, spots and colourful patterns. Play around with the bug's eyes and add lashes and dots around them.

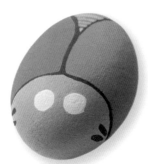

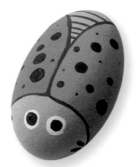

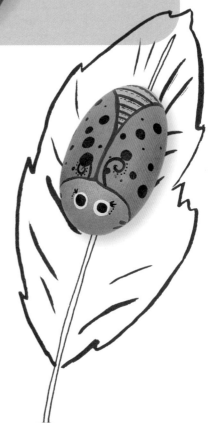

4 Outline the wings with a fine line of red paint and add horizontal lines on the back part of the body. Add two small petal shapes on either side of the bug's face.

5 Using black paint, add big and small spots on the wings. Add black spots to the eyes.

6 Finally, add two spiralled antennae, one on each wing. Add some eyelashes to the eyes. Allow to dry and then add a layer of varnish.

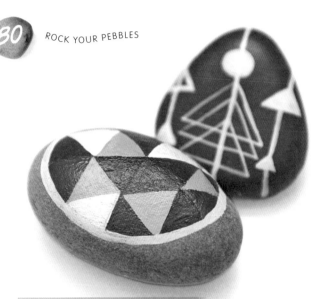

YOU WILL NEED

- ☑ Oval-shaped pebble
- ☑ Damp cloth
- ☑ White chalk
- ☑ Red, brown and white craft paint
- ☑ Paintbrushes
- ☑ White marker
- ☑ Varnish

TRY TRIANGLES

Triangles can look great on pebbles, creating an interesting contrast between the sharpness of the angles and the roundness of the pebble. Additionally, triangles can make brilliant geometric patterns and designs, either alone or combined with other shapes.

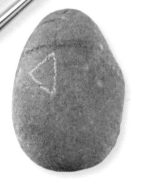

1 Choose a smooth, oval-shaped pebble and clean it with a damp cloth. Using the chalk, draw one triangle anywhere on your pebble; it doesn't matter where this pattern starts.

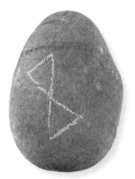

2 Draw another triangle with one of its points touching one of the points of your first triangle. It should look like a simple bow tie.

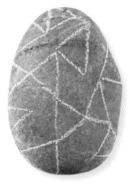

3 Repeat this pattern all over the pebble, making sure the triangles touch each other at some point.

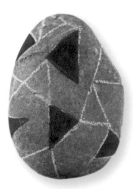

4 Fill in some of the triangles with red paint, leaving some triangles empty for the other two colours.

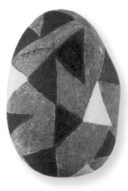

5 Fill in the remaining triangles with white and brown paint.

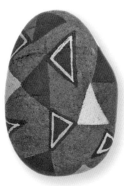

6 As a finishing touch, use a white marker to draw a triangle outline inside the red triangles. Once dry, varnish your pebble all over.

VARIATIONS Try these triangles out

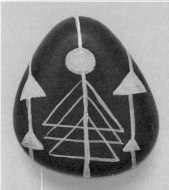

∧ **Get Geometrical**
Using only one colour and a white marker pen, you can create a simple and striking geometrical design. Draw three vertical lines and some triangles along the lines. A triangular pebble would be perfect for this pattern.

∨ **Triangles and More**
Incorporate other shapes including lines, circles and dots to create this primitive triangular pattern.

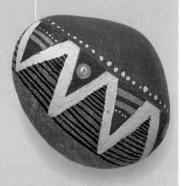

∨ **Tessellating Triangles**
Create a repetitive triangular pattern enclosed in an oval on the front of your pebble. Make use of a variety of colours – the more, the better!

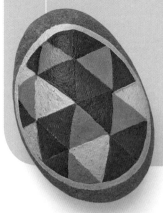

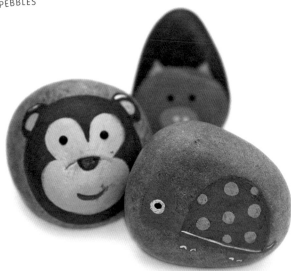

ANIMAL FAVOURITES

We all have a favourite animal – whether it's a pet, an animal we enjoyed drawing as a kid or even an animal that we feel represents ourselves! These illustrated pebbles are really charming and a fun way to create an animal rock without having to hunt for that perfectly shaped stone for a 3D animal.

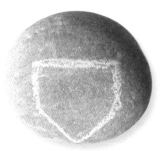

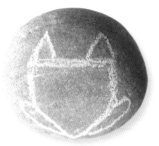

1 To paint the fox, choose a round pebble with a smooth surface and clean it with a damp cloth. Use chalk to sketch a rectangle towards the centre of your pebble. Then add a triangle at the bottom of the rectangle to make the face of a fox.

2 Add two triangular ears on top and add the cheeks on each side of the bottom triangle. This is the basic shape for your foxy friend.

3 Now that the sketch is ready, paint the fox using brown for the face and white paint for the cheeks.

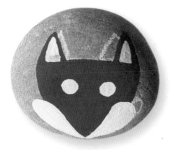

4 Using white paint, add two small triangular shapes inside the ears and two circles for the eyes.

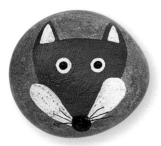

5 Use the 3D liner to make black blobs inside the eyes and a bigger one for the nose. Add whiskers with black paint or the pen. Allow to dry, rub off any visible chalk and then add a layer of varnish.

VARIATIONS Which one's your favourite?

Pinky Pig >

Chubby and a bit smelly, pigs are still adorable and are very easy to paint! Using a dark pebble will make your animal stand out more.

OINK

< Mister Crocs

An elongated pebble is perfect for this so you can fit in the crocodile's huge jaws.

∨ Slow and Steady Shelly

Why not try painting a whole animal, like Shelly, rather than just a face? Decorate her shell with spots or other patterns.

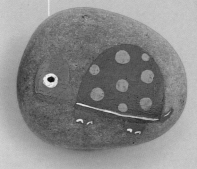

Cheeky Charlie ∧

It's actually really easy to create this cheeky monkey character. Focus on the main shapes that make up his face, and he'll soon come to life.

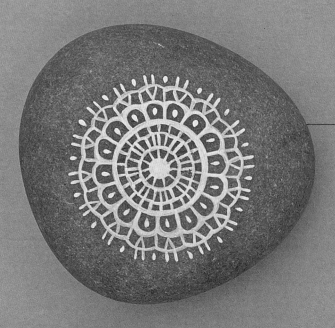

< Clean and Classic

This design is very effective on smaller, rounder pebbles. Just use a fine brush and work slowly and precisely to build up your mandala. The neutral colours look natural and stylish. If you are concerned about your brush control, you could always use a white marker pen to draw the very fine lines.

> Striking Contrast

Paint a circle in black paint, let it dry and then very carefully paint your mandala in white on the top. Black and white make for a very striking variation of this design.

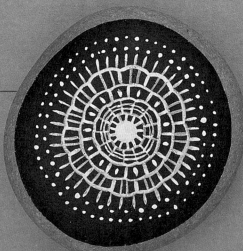

MAKING MANDALAS

Mandalas are beautiful and often incredibly intricate designs, and their circular shape means they're perfectly suited for painting on rocks. You need a lot of patience and a very steady hand, but once finished, these painted rocks would look beautiful displayed in

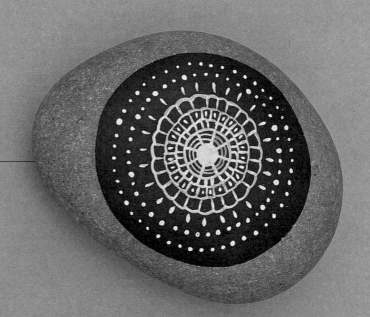

> **Make a Circle from an Oval**

If you have chosen a pebble that is oval in shape, you can paint a black circle in the centre to form your mandala. Leaving the natural stone visible around the edges of your design will create a nice contrast.

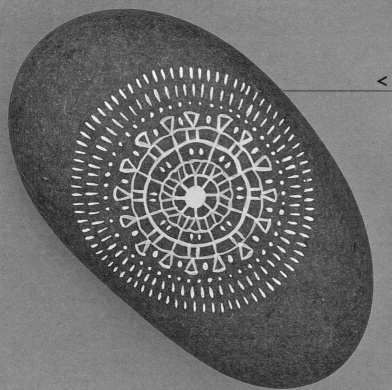

< **Circles and Symmetry**

Find a large, dark-coloured stone and use white paint as a beautiful contrast. Start with a small circle at the centre of your mandala and gradually add lines, dashes and spots, joining some of these to create a continuous circular design. Your finished mandala would make a striking ornament on a bookshelf or mantelpiece, or you could use it as a beautiful paperweight.

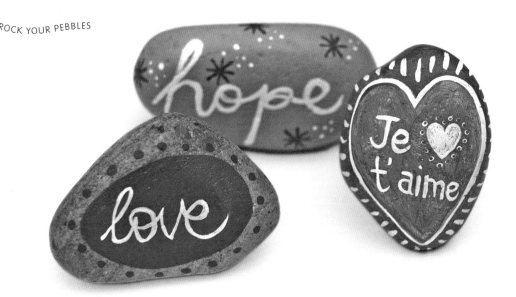

YOU WILL NEED

- ☑ Two pebbles, big enough to fit your chosen words
- ☑ Damp cloth
- ☑ Red, green and white craft paint
- ☑ Paintbrushes
- ☑ White chalk
- ☑ White marker pen (optional)
- ☑ Varnish

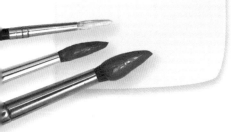

FROM ME TO YOU

Pebbles decorated with names, words or quotes that have a special meaning make fantastic tokens and really thoughtful gifts. Why not make a matching pair as demonstrated here, and give one to a loved one and keep its sister pebble for yourself? They can also be lovely just to keep for yourself – place them next to the candles in your living room or carry them in your purse as a lucky charm. Painting cursive script can be tricky to get right; sketching your word in chalk first is a good way to avoid mistakes.

1 Choose your pebbles, and clean them with a damp cloth. Make sure they are big enough to fit your chosen words. With white chalk, sketch an oval shape on each pebble, taking up most of the available space on the surface. Fill in the circles using complementary but not matching colours of craft paint. Let the paint dry and then gently rub off any visible chalk.

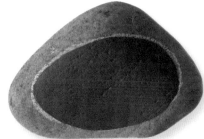
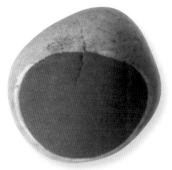

VARIATIONS Make somebody's day with these thoughtful pebble messages

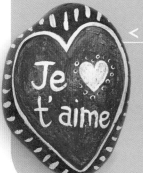

< Be Mine?

Bored of the same old Valentine's cards? Express your love in a unique way and create the perfect personalised gift. Why even wait until 14th February? Tell that special someone how you feel today.

> Homemade Mantra

Your pebble messages needn't be for a particular occasion. Why not give a token of hope to keep them positive every day – a powerful message that can just be popped in a pocket!

2 Again using the chalk, write the words 'love' and 'peace' on your pebbles. You can rub off whatever you write in chalk so experiment with fonts and styles, upper or lower case, block letters or cursive – don't be shy!

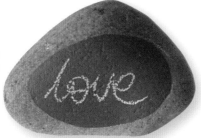
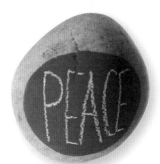

3 Trace over the chalk letters with white paint or a white marker pen to make your words bolder and brighter. Work slowly and keep your lettering neat. Go over for a second layer if needed. Once dry, gently rub off any visible chalk.

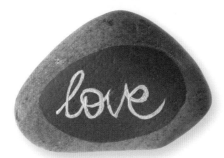
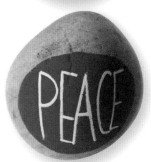

4 Finally, decorate your pebble messages by adding dots or lines in the other colour around the edge of the oval shape. Varnish when dry.

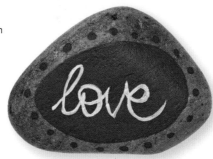
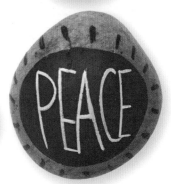

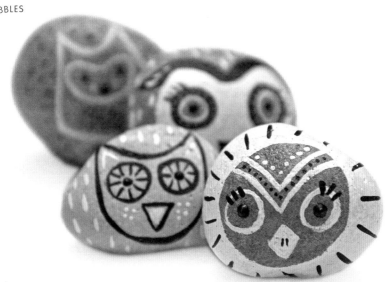

YOU WILL NEED

- ☑ Round, flat pebble
- ☑ Damp cloth
- ☑ White chalk
- ☑ White and black craft paint
- ☑ Paintbrush
- ☑ Black marker pen (optional)
- ☑ Black 3D liner
- ☑ Varnish

HOOT YOUR PEBBLES

You can paint really effective owl faces on your pebbles, using just black and white linework – with plenty of fun guaranteed. Using a palette of only black and white gives a clean, graphic look that makes these owl portrait pebbles fantastic for using as house decorations.

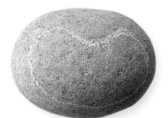

1 Choose a round, flat pebble and clean with a damp cloth. Sketch a 'bean' shape in the centre of your pebble using white chalk.

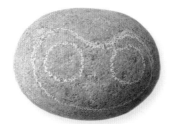

2 Add two circles on each side for the owl's eyes.

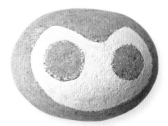

3 Paint the inside of the shape white, leaving the eyes unpainted.

VARIATIONS You'll have a hoot with these birds of a feather

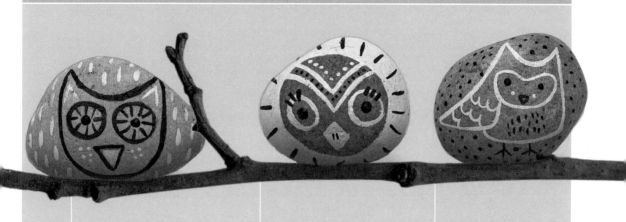

A Bird's Eye View
Make the head a different shape with pointed ears. These huge eyes have an almost hypnotic effect.

Luna the Night Owl
Make the head more circular and get creative with eyelashes, background spots or lines and other patterns.

Wing It
Now that you know how to draw an owl head on a pebble, why not add a body? Easy, isn't it? Find other full-body owls on pages 40–41.

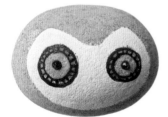

4 Focus on the eyes by outlining a double border with black paint or a marker pen. Connect the two circles with small lines all the way around. Add dots of black 3D liner in the centre of the eyes.

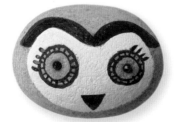

5 Now add some definition to the top of the owl's head by adding a thick black line. Add a triangular beak and some eyelashes too.

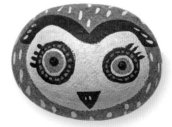

6 Finally, add some white 'feathery' lines all over the pebble. Once dry, varnish your pebble completely.

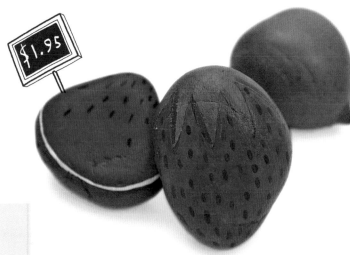

YOU WILL NEED

- ☑ Triangular pebble
- ☑ Damp cloth
- ☑ White chalk
- ☑ Red, green, dark red and dark green craft paint
- ☑ Paintbrushes
- ☑ Varnish

TUTTI FRUTTI

If you want something a bit more complex than illustrated fruits (pages 38–39), this is the project for you – but it will take a bit of careful rock hunting to find the perfect shape for a specific piece of fruit. Instead, let the shapes of pebbles you find inspire you to create certain fruits. A perfectly round pebble can be easily transformed into an orange, while a triangular shape can remind us of a sweet and juicy strawberry!

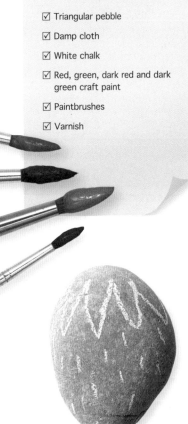

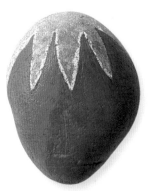

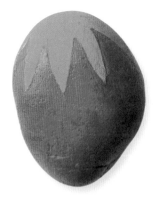

1 Choose a triangular pebble, similar to a strawberry shape, and clean it with a damp cloth. Sketch out the green sepals by adding leaf-like zigzag shapes with chalk around the top of the pebble.

2 Paint the lower part of your pebble in red paint, applying a second layer if necessary. You may want to paint one side and wait for it to dry before turning the stone over to paint the reverse.

3 Now paint the sepals using green paint.

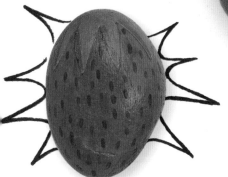

4 Using dark red paint, randomly add some short lines over the red part of the strawberry to represent the seeds.

5 Using a slightly darker green paint, create a shadowy effect on the sepals by adding a line on each 'leaf'. Allow to dry completely and then add a layer of varnish.

VARIATIONS These look good enough to eat!

A Citrus Twist

It's common to find a pebble that's almost perfect for a piece of fruit, but may have a feature or two missing. But don't worry! Make use of wood filler to add any details you like, such as the pointed upper part of this green lime!

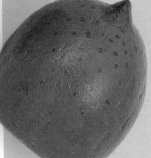

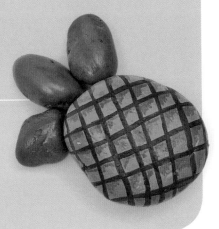

Mouthwateringly Good

This is a great opportunity to make use of odd-shaped pebbles like this one. By using green paint for the rind of the fruit and red for the inside, you can create the perfect 3D slice of watermelon! The black pips are a great finishing touch.

Pineapple Puzzle >

There's no need to limit yourself to one stone. This pineapple is made up of four different pebbles. Use tiny pebbles alongside bigger ones to create more realistic rocky fruits.

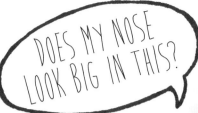

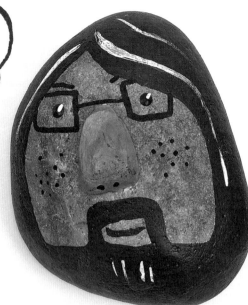

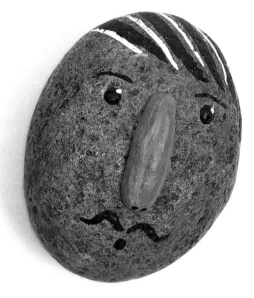

> ## Hey, Big Nose!

Start by drawing a simple portrait using just black paint or marker pen with a few white highlights. Then use wood filler to add a massive, comical nose to the centre of the face. This is a really fun way to make a cheeky caricature of someone you know. Or stay on the safe side and play around with the hair, beard and other features to create some fun original characters. (Don't forget to wear plastic gloves when using wood filler.)

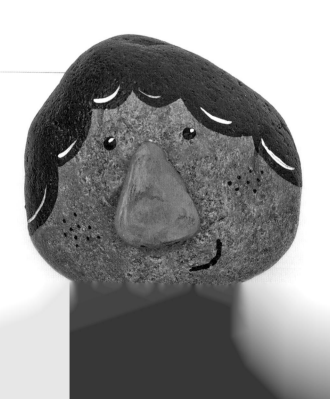

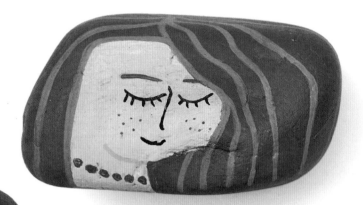

< Hair-Raising Ideas

For a more flattering rock representation of your friends and family, focus on the hair. Make use of the whole of the surface of the pebble, but keep the face and the features relatively small and delicate. The shapes of the pebbles you find could inspire you to create characters with some wild and wacky hairstyles: afros, beehives or even mohawks!

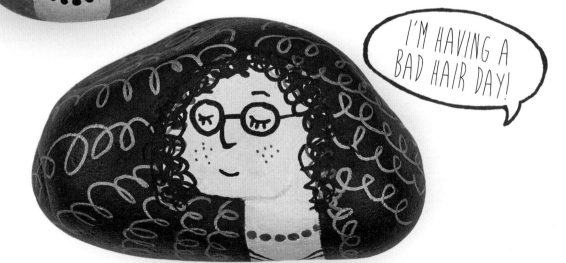

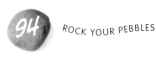

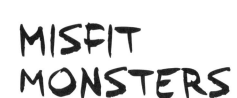

MISFIT MONSTERS

You don't have to be constrained by the stones that you find or even buy. You can use wood filler to make a 'rock' of any shape that you can think of (see page 21). Use these ideas to bring to life the gruesomest goblins you can imagine with rock art.

YOU WILL NEED

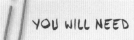

- ☑ Pebble
- ☑ Damp cloth
- ☑ Plastic gloves
- ☑ Wood filler
- ☑ Dark blue, white, black and light blue craft paint
- ☑ Paintbrushes
- ☑ White chalk
- ☑ Varnish

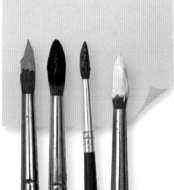

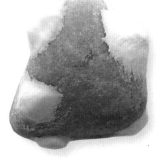

1 Clean your pebble with a damp cloth and put on a pair of plastic gloves. Apply wood filler blobs to your pebble to form your basic monster shape, ensuring he stands upright. Let it dry for about eight hours.

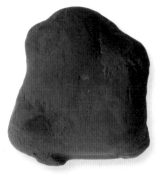

2 When the wood filler is completely dry, paint the whole pebble in dark blue paint. You may want to paint one side, let it dry and then turn over to paint the reverse.

VARIATIONS Try these other wacky wood-filler weirdos

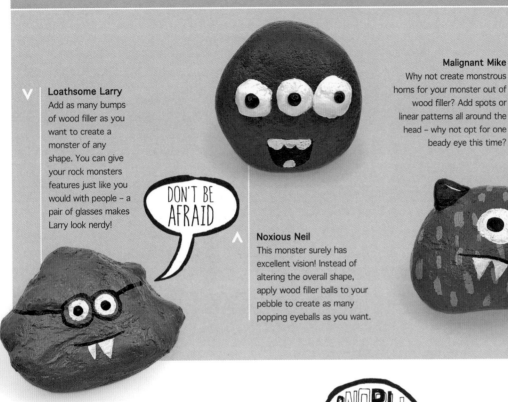

Loathsome Larry
Add as many bumps of wood filler as you want to create a monster of any shape. You can give your rock monsters features just like you would with people – a pair of glasses makes Larry look nerdy!

DON'T BE AFRAID

Noxious Neil
This monster surely has excellent vision! Instead of altering the overall shape, apply wood filler balls to your pebble to create as many popping eyeballs as you want.

Malignant Mike
Why not create monstrous horns for your monster out of wood filler? Add spots or linear patterns all around the head – why not opt for one beady eye this time?

SNARL!

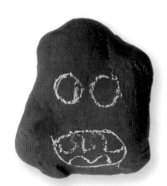

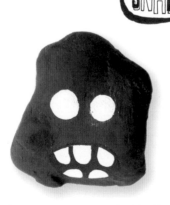

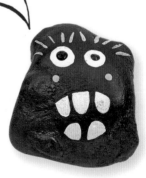

3 Use the chalk to sketch a pair of big round eyes and a huge open mouth with uneven teeth.

4 Paint the eyes and teeth with white paint. Fill in the remaining parts of the mouth with black paint.

5 Add black dots to the centre of the eyes. Add further decoration to your monster using light blue paint. Once dry, apply a coat of varnish.

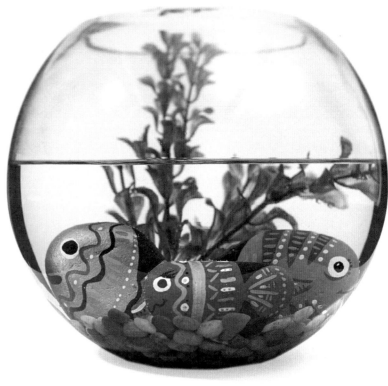

YOU WILL NEED

- ☑ Oval pebble
- ☑ Damp cloth
- ☑ White chalk
- ☑ Orange, white, black, red and dark blue craft paint
- ☑ Paintbrushes
- ☑ Varnish

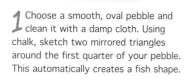

FISH TAILS

These elaborate fish are proud to show off their beautifully decorated tails (technically called caudal fins). The trick is to add two mirrored dark triangles, which will create the appearance and shape of your fish's tail. Combined with the ideas on pages 30–31, 48–49 and 66–67, these would look great decorating any bathroom or fish tank.

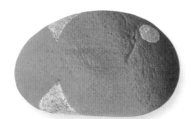

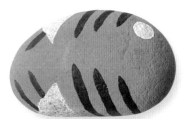

1 Choose a smooth, oval pebble and clean it with a damp cloth. Using chalk, sketch two mirrored triangles around the first quarter of your pebble. This automatically creates a fish shape.

2 Fill in the rest of the surface of the pebble using orange paint and then, when dry, paint a round eye in white. If you want to paint your whole pebble, paint one side and wait for it to dry before painting the other side.

3 Starting at the top of the pebble, add black lines, which stop just before the centre. Do the same at the bottom, painting your line upwards. Add smaller lines on the tail.

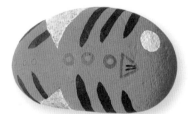

4 Decorate your fish by adding red circles along the centre of the fish. Add a small triangular pectoral fin close to the eyes.

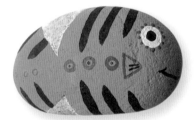

5 Next, bring your fish to life by adding a black dot in the centre of the eye and painting the mouth. Add small red dots around the eye.

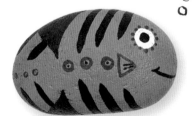

6 Finally, fill in the missing triangles to define the shape of your fish using dark blue or black paint. Allow to dry and then add a layer of varnish.

VARIATIONS There's plenty more fish in the sea!

Coral the Clownfish >

Experiment with a different selection of colours and play around with patterns. Remember, they don't have to be realistic.

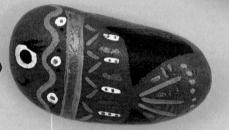

Coy Little Koi

Tiny pebbles can also be used for painting fish. Use a fine brush with a steady hand. These look particularly great in fish tanks.

Mr. Goldy Fish >

Make way for the majestic golden fish. Use gold paint to make your fish look lovely and shiny and add curvy lines to decorate your fish!

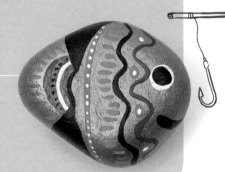

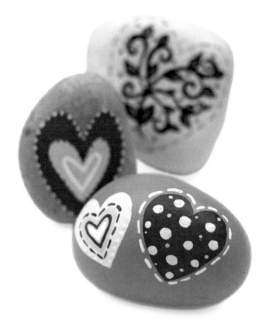

LOVE HEARTS

Hearts painted on pebbles create a cosy, quaint feeling. Keep them in your own home, making it look and feel warmer. Or why not give someone a heart charm to show them you're thinking of them – you could even add a message (see pages 86–87).

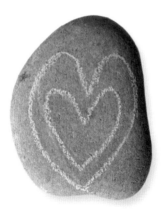

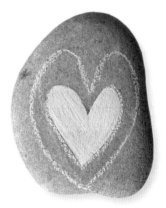

1 Choose an oval pebble and clean with a damp cloth. Using chalk, draw a large heart then sketch a smaller one inside of it.

2 Paint the inner heart in a light blue. Give it two coats if needed.

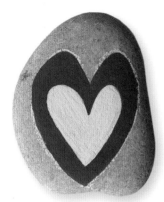 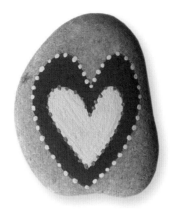 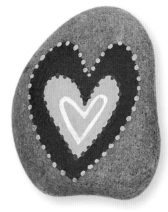

3 Use the red paint to paint the outer heart, applying a second layer if necessary. Once dry, carefully rub off any chalk that is still visible.

4 Add a dotted outline around the outside of the larger heart with light blue paint. Then add dark blue dots around the outside of the inner heart.

5 As a finishing touch, paint a small heart outline inside the smaller heart using white paint. Allow to dry and then add a layer of varnish.

VARIATIONS Vary these designs to your heart's content

Heart to Heart
Paint as many hearts as you want on your pebble! Alternate the colours among the hearts, sticking to a basic colour scheme. You can alter this colour scheme of pale yellow, red and blue to suit your home or the chosen recipient.

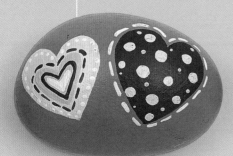

A Heart of Stone
Create a pretty motif inside the heart, such as a tree with sprouting leaves or flowers. Add dotted lines around the outside of the main heart to add to the folky design.

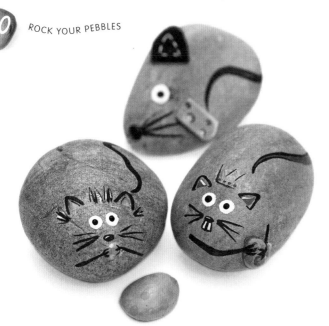

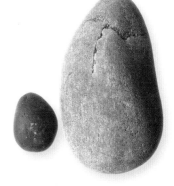

1 Select the pebbles for your mouse and cheese, and clean them both with a damp cloth.

MICE 'N' CHEESE

The colour and shape of most pebbles lend themselves perfectly to creating mouse characters. You don't even have to paint your pebble: a simple face and a tail, and instant mouse! The addition of cheese gives your pebble mouse projects a fun twist, and there are so many ways to do it. Find out how here!

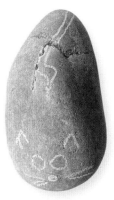

2 Using white chalk, sketch a nose, some whiskers, a pair of eyes and some pointed ears on the larger pebble. Sketch a tail, starting from the very top of the pebble.

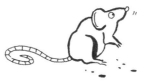

YOU WILL NEED

- ☑ One large oval pebble and one tiny round pebble
- ☑ Damp cloth
- ☑ White chalk
- ☑ Black, white, grey, yellow and mustard craft paint
- ☑ Paintbrushes
- ☑ Black fine liner (optional)
- ☑ Varnish

VARIATIONS Play around with these while the cat's away

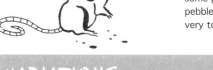

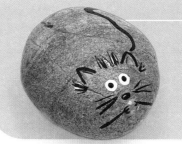

< **Say Cheese!**

Use a round pebble to create your own cute, chubby mouse character. This time use wood filler to add some cheese just over his mouth. Add two thin black hands holding that delicious cheese!

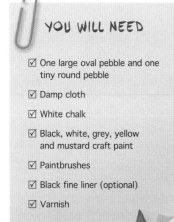

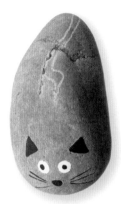 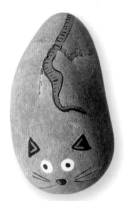 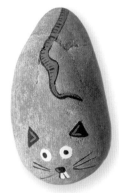

3 When you are happy with the face and tail, fill in the features using black and white paint. You may find it easier to draw the fine whiskers using a black fine liner pen.

4 Next, paint the twirling tail using grey paint. Outline the tail in black paint or fine liner, and add some lines to create a 3D effect. Paint some grey on the sides of the ears too.

5 Add a pair of white teeth just below the nose and outline in black paint or fine liner. You've finished your mouse!

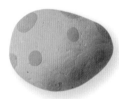

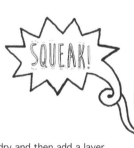

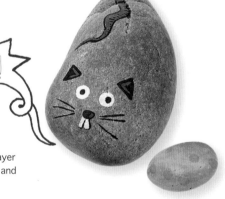

6 Now your mouse is ready to eat some cheese! Paint the small pebble with yellow paint and, once dry, add some random spots with mustard paint to make it look like cheese.

7 Allow to dry and then add a layer of varnish to both the mouse and the cheese.

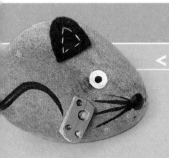

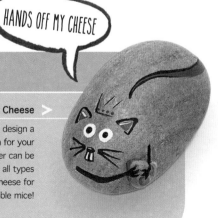

< Crafty Critter

If you are super crafty, try adding in different materials: make some ears from black felt and stick them onto the pebble using PVA glue. Cut a small piece from a lolly stick, paint it yellow and attach it next to the mouse's whiskers.

King of Cheese >

Use gold paint to design a little crown for your mouse. Wood filler can be used to make all types and sizes of cheese for your pebble mice!

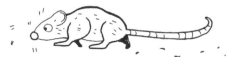

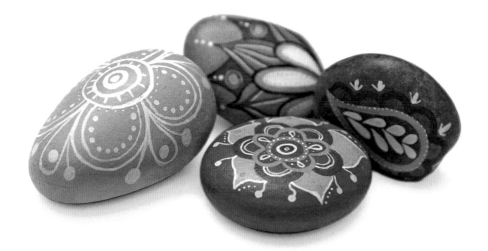

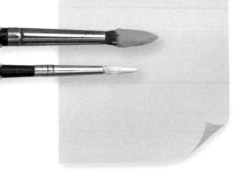

GET FOLKY

The folky patterns you can come up with are endless! Here you'll find some charming designs that can be applied to your pebbles in just a few minutes to make beautiful decorative stones. Make use of coloured patterns to match your home, or try black or white outlines for a simple, stylish look.

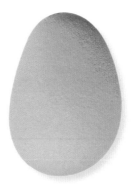

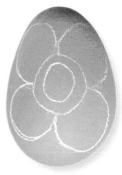

1 Choose a smooth, round pebble, and clean it with a damp cloth. Paint the whole pebble with light blue paint, making sure you cover the back of the pebble. Give it a second coat if you think the paint is not thick enough.

2 Once the paint is dry, use the chalk to draw two concentric circles in the centre of the blue pebble. Draw petal-like semicircles around the central circle, creating a flower effect.

VARIATIONS Try out these folky finishes

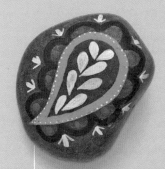

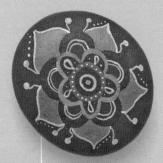

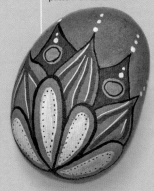

Leafy Layers
Paint different layers of leaves using various colours. Yellows, reds and greens will give this pattern an autumnal feel.

Pretty in Paisley
Why not make use of the natural texture and colours of your pebble? Paint a paisley design onto your pebble without applying any background colour. You will see how your design stands out even more!

Colour Me Vibrant
Colour is always welcome in folk culture. Create similar flower designs using vibrant orange, purple, turquoise and yellow. Add white outlines with a white marker or paint to make the design pop.

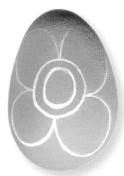

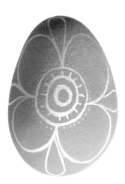

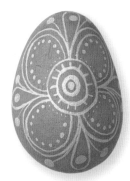

3 With your white marker or paint, trace over the chalk lines to start forming your folky flower.

4 Continue to add more details with your white marker or paint. Add small leaves in between the petals, and details to the centre circle.

5 Add dots or patterns and further embellishment around your design to give it that folky style. Once dry, rub off the remaining chalk with your fingers. Add a layer of varnish to finish.

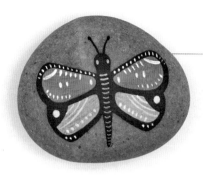

Float Like a Butterfly

Try combining two complementary colours such as orange and blue on your butterfly's wings. Paint the butterfly silhouette in black first and then, once dry, add the colours on top. Finish your design with white details. You could even use four colours, a different colour on each wing, for an ineresting, asymmetrical design.

Wings of White

If you have a particularly small stone, keep the butterfly design clean and uncomplicated. White works so well against a taupe-coloured stone for a natural effect. An elongated body and shallow wings will begin to transform your butterfly into a dragonfly.

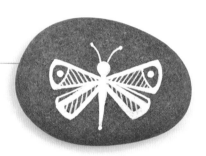

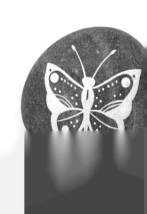

Social Butterfly

When you're getting started, paint a basic butterfly silhouette in black and then add the colour and details afterwards – choose a favourite colour for the wings and keep the design fairly simple. A few of these sweet pebbles in different colours would look great as magnets holding up photographs on a refrigerator door.

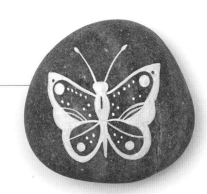

> **Madame Butterfly**

For a striking butterfly design, stick to one colour but add lots of detailing. Start with the body and then move on to the basic shape of wings, finishing with the details. An intricate white butterfly on a natural, flat stone would be great as a pendant. Drill the hole in the pebble before painting, or buy predrilled pebbles.

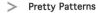

< **Minuscule Minibeasts**

Tiny stones require less complex designs, so keep the butterfly shape very simple and then add a bright colour with a few white details for interest. This teeny pebble would make a lovely lucky charm.

> **Pretty Patterns**

You don't need lots of colours to create an interesting design. Paint a basic butterfly shape and then fill in the details afterwards. Use spots, stripes, dashes, lines or any other patterns you can think of for a pretty effect.

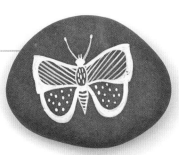

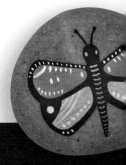

Butterflies are common in design motifs because they are beautiful, fragile, appealingly symmetrical, dainty, colourful, evocative of summer days, and symbolic of growth and metamorphosis. Painted butterfly motifs could be used in almost any rock art project – use some of these designs as your inspiration.

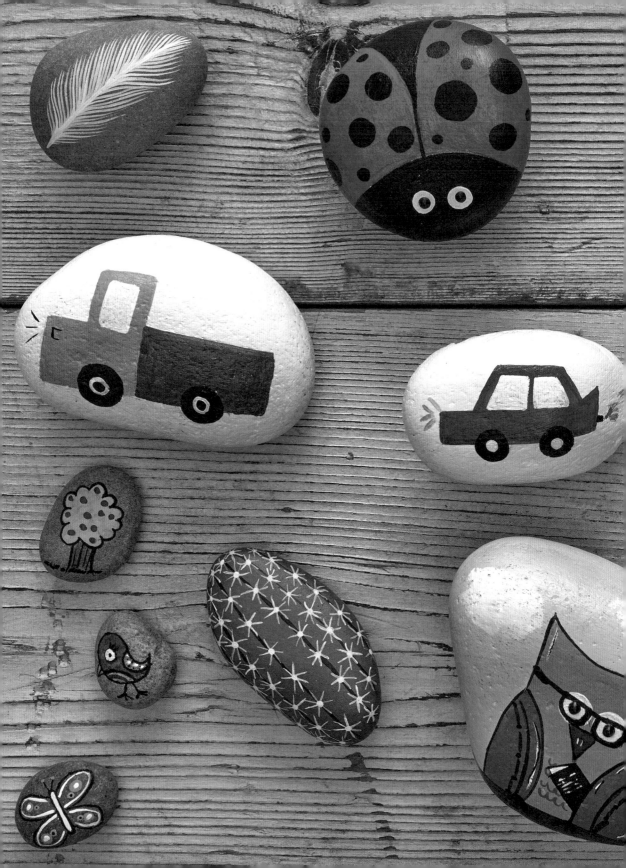

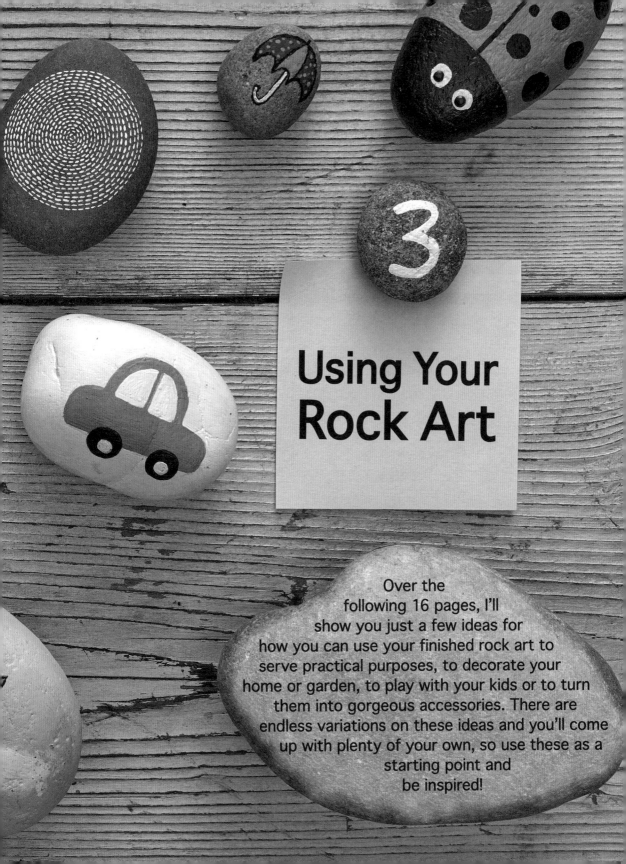

Using Your Rock Art

Over the following 16 pages, I'll show you just a few ideas for how you can use your finished rock art to serve practical purposes, to decorate your home or garden, to play with your kids or to turn them into gorgeous accessories. There are endless variations on these ideas and you'll come up with plenty of your own, so use these as a starting point and be inspired!

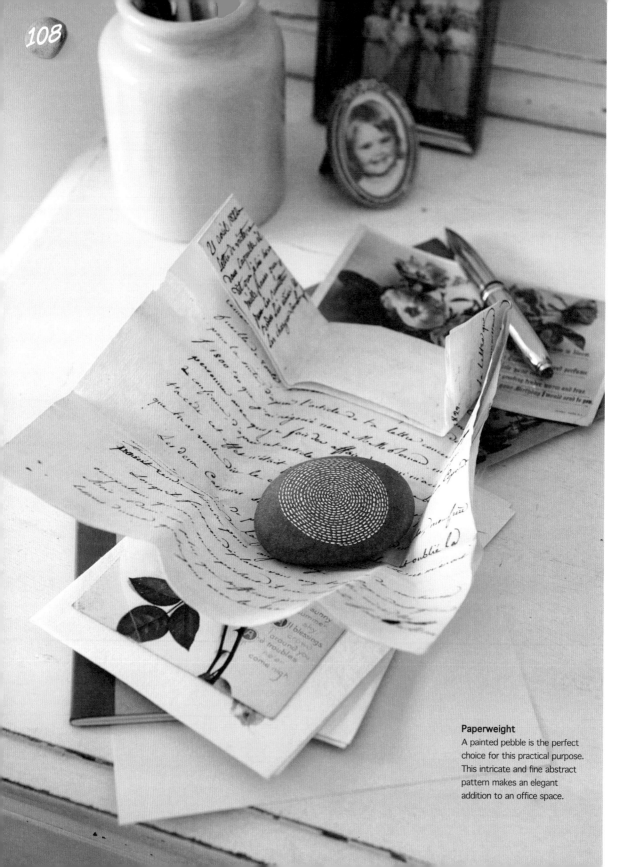

Paperweight
A painted pebble is the perfect choice for this practical purpose. This intricate and fine abstract pattern makes an elegant addition to an office space.

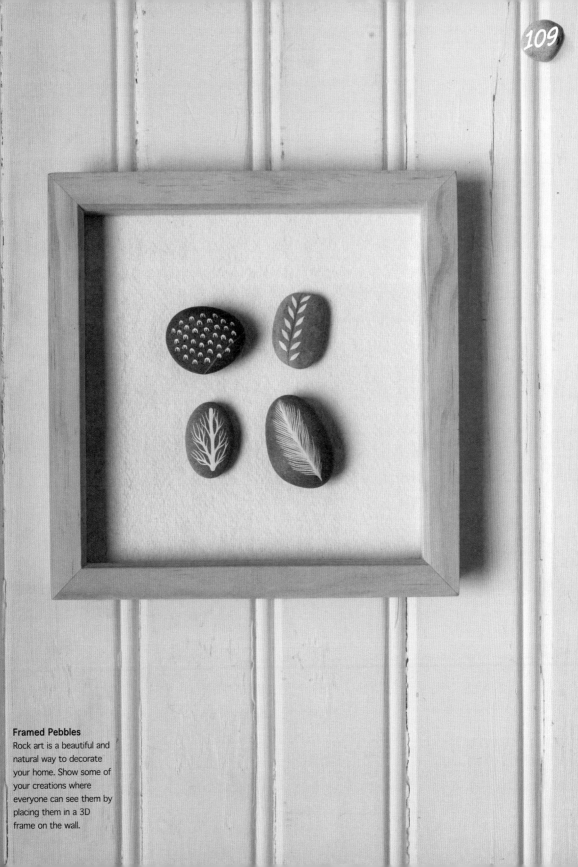

Framed Pebbles

Rock art is a beautiful and natural way to decorate your home. Show some of your creations where everyone can see them by placing them in a 3D frame on the wall.

THE TALE OF PETER RABBIT
THE TALE OF SQUIRREL NUTKIN
THE TAILOR OF GLOUCESTER
THE TALE OF BENJAMIN BUNNY
THE TALE OF TWO BAD MICE
THE TALE OF MR. JEREMY FISHER
THE TALE OF TOM KITTEN

1	2	3	4	5		7	8	10
WARNE	WARNE	WARNE	WARNE	WARNE		WARNE	WARNE	WARNE

Bookends

Transform two similar-size stones into a pair of beautiful bookends. Keep your shelves tidy and admire them every time you reach for a good book.

THE TALE OF MRS. TITTLEMOUSE

THE TALE OF JOHNNY TOWN-MOUSE

THE TALE OF MR. TOD

THE TALE OF PIGLING BLAND

THE TALE OF LITTLE PIG ROBINSON

THE TALE OF TIMMY TIPTOES

THE TALE OF
TIMMY TIPTOES

13 WARNE

14 WARNE

WARNE

15 WARNE

19 WARNE

12 WARNE

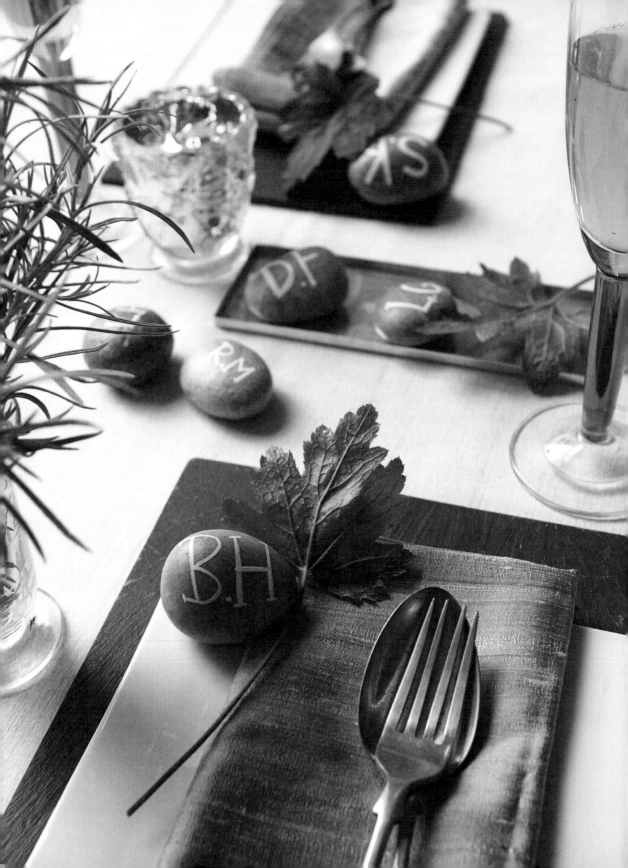

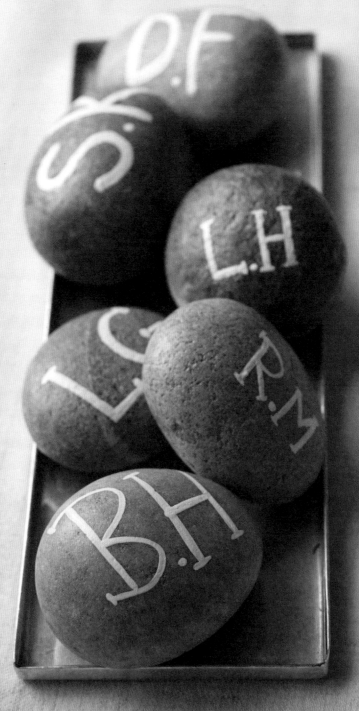

Place Names
Give your wedding, dinner party or Christmas table a unique and personal touch by using these initialled stones to mark each of your guests' places.

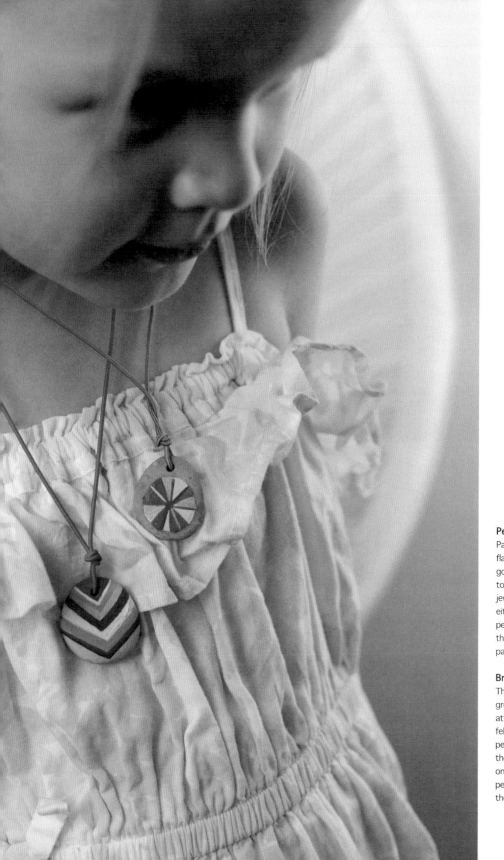

Pendants

Paint abstract designs on flat, smooth pebbles for a gorgeous and simple way to create customised jewellery. You will need to either buy predrilled pebbles or carefully drill the holes yourself (see pages 22–23).

Brooches

These cute accessories look great and can be made by attaching a piece of thick felt to the back of your pebble with super glue, and then stitching a brooch pin onto the fabric. Small pebbles like these will work the best.

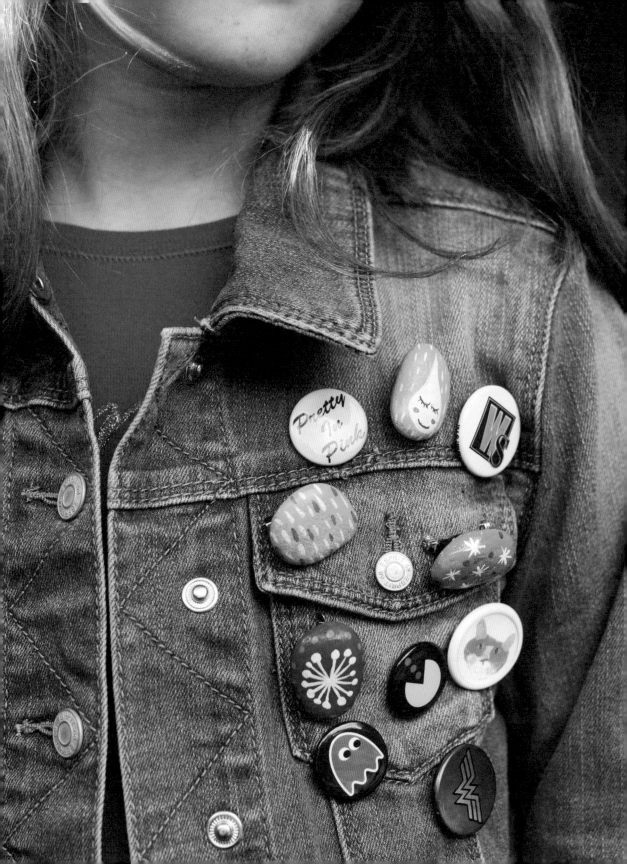

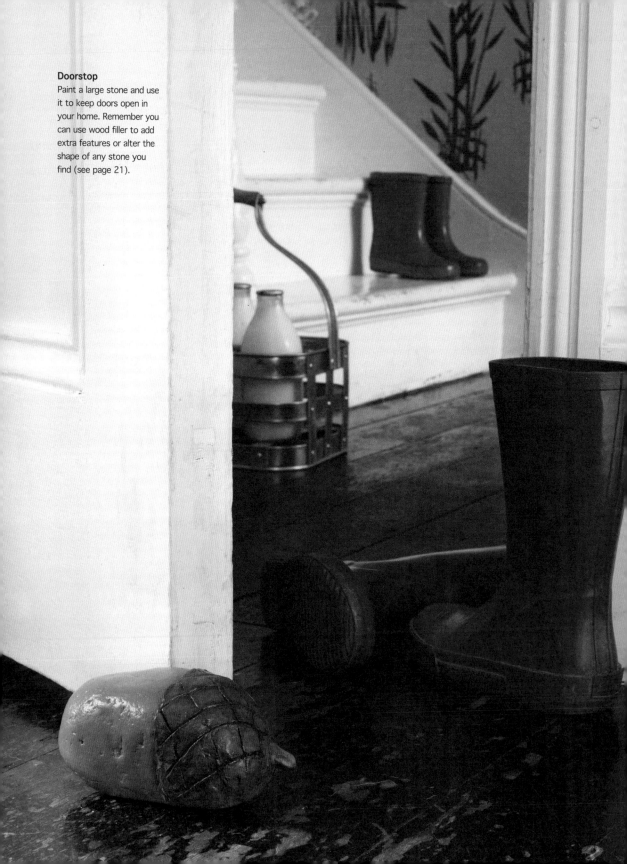

Doorstop
Paint a large stone and use
it to keep doors open in
your home. Remember you
can use wood filler to add
extra features or alter the
shape of any stone you
find (see page 21).

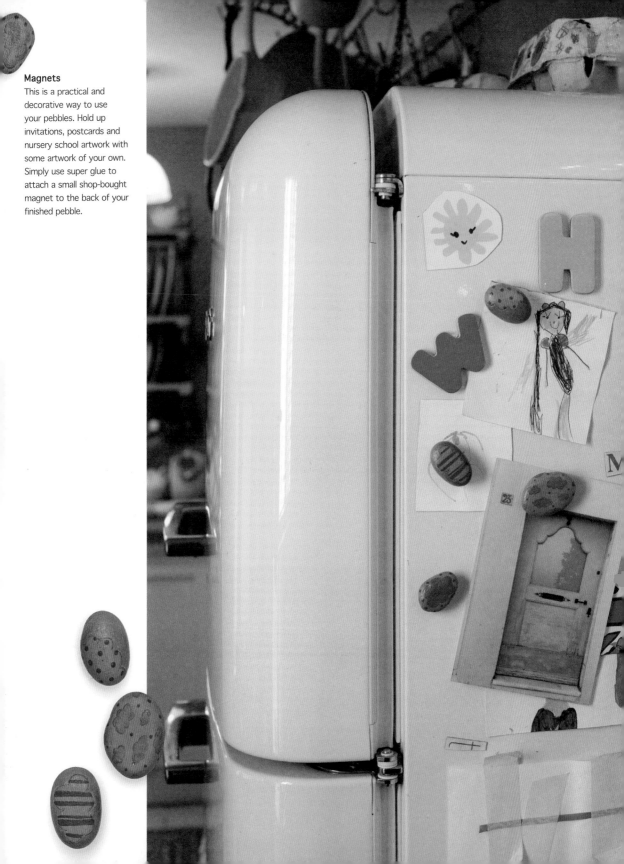

Magnets

This is a practical and decorative way to use your pebbles. Hold up invitations, postcards and nursery school artwork with some artwork of your own. Simply use super glue to attach a small shop-bought magnet to the back of your finished pebble.

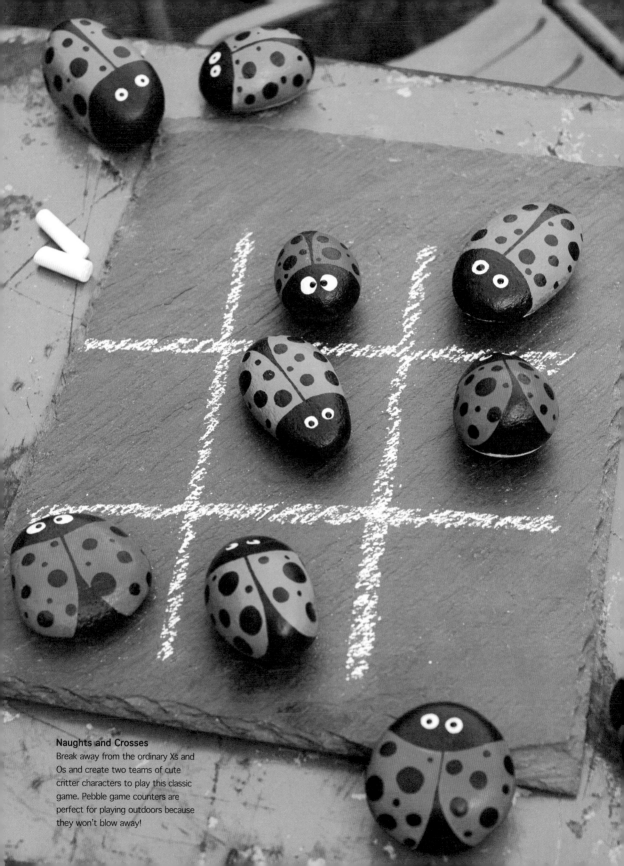

Naughts and Crosses
Break away from the ordinary Xs and
Os and create two teams of cute
critter characters to play this classic
game. Pebble game counters are
perfect for playing outdoors because
they won't blow away!

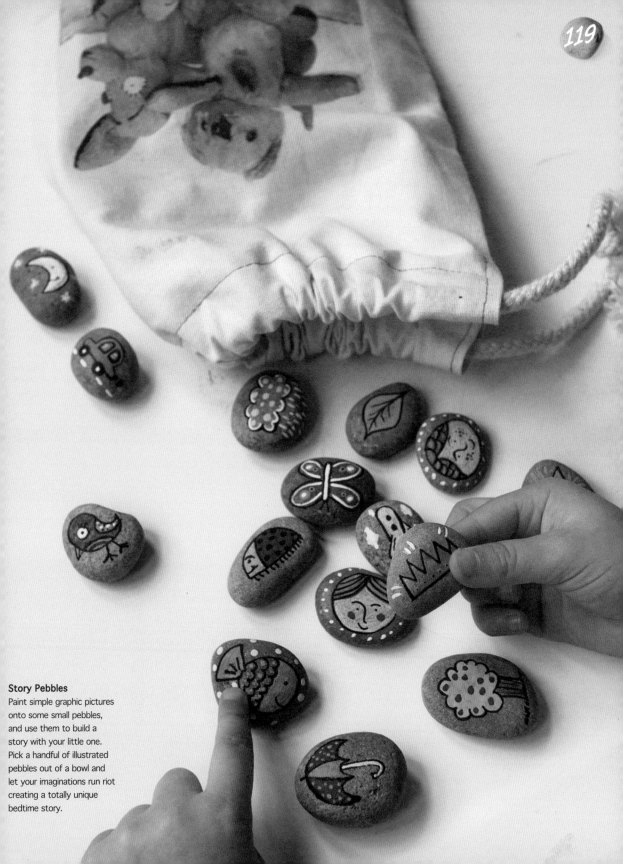

Story Pebbles
Paint simple graphic pictures
onto some small pebbles,
and use them to build a
story with your little one.
Pick a handful of illustrated
pebbles out of a bowl and
let your imaginations run riot
creating a totally unique
bedtime story.

Toy Cars

There's no need to spend money on expensive plastic toys. Painted stones make great toy cars, and with just a Sharpie and some paper, you can create a whole town. Plus, creating the cars becomes a fun activity as well!

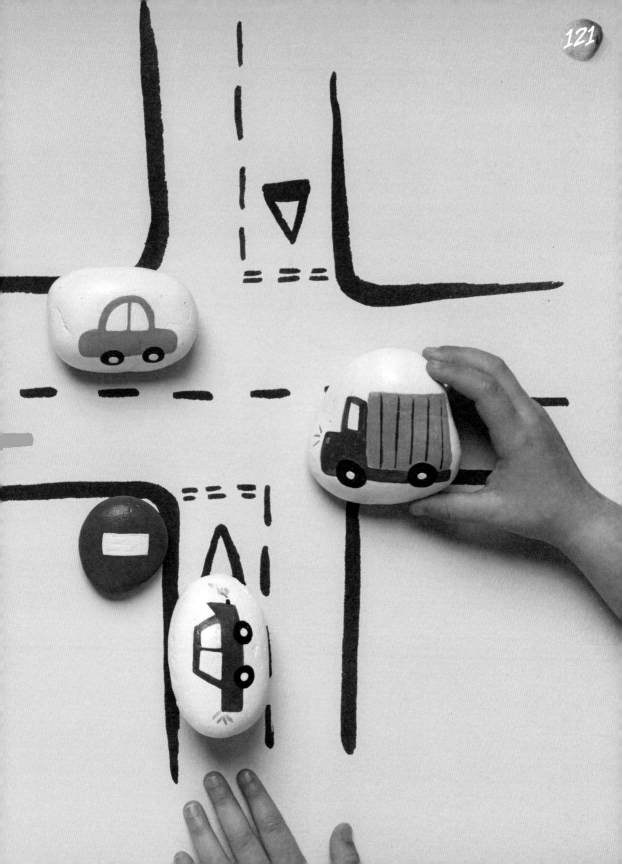

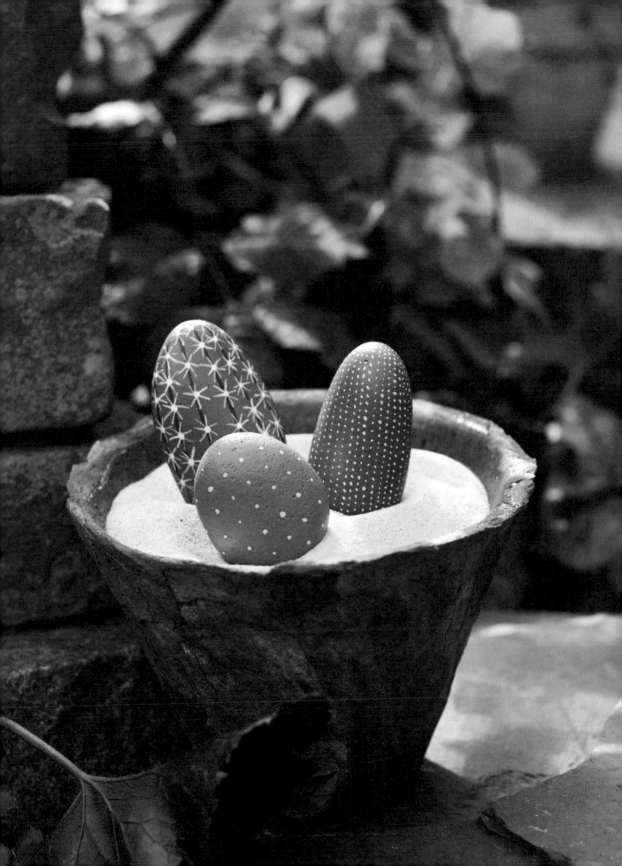

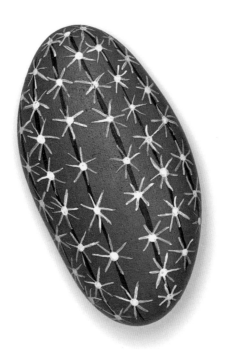

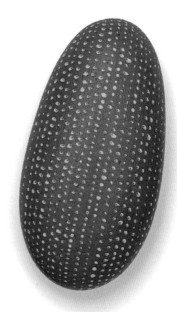

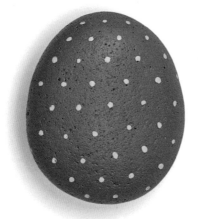

Garden Ornaments

Don't keep your rock art creations indoors – they make fantastic, durable garden ornaments, too. Make a feature of them (like these cacti), nestle some in your flowerbeds or plant pots, or try using them as unique plant labels for your herb garden.

INDEX

INDEX

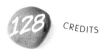

CREDITS

To learn more about the author, visit her website at
www.denisescicluna.com.

The author and Quarto would like to thank Natasha Newton who supplied
the rock art on pages 36–37, 52–53, 84–85, 104–105, 108–109 and
122–123. Learn more about Natasha at *www.natasha-newton.co.uk*.

Quarto would like to thank the following for supplying images for
inclusion in the book:

Galea, Stephanie, *www.stephaniegalea.com*, p.7
Perola, Preto, *Shutterstock.com*, pp.10–11
Rauski, Ivana, *Shutterstock.com*, pp.12t, 13
Naluwan, *Shutterstock.com*, p.12b
Pukach, *Shutterstock.com*, p.12m
Ingugulija, *Shutterstock.com*, p.27

All step-by-step and other images are the copyright of
Quarto Publishing plc.

The information on drilling holes in pebbles on pages 22–23 is based on
Authentic Arts blogger Jenny Hoople's online tutorial 'How to drill small
beach stones' (*http://jennyhoople.com/blog/how-to-drill-small-beach-
stones*). Thanks to Jenny for answering our questions on this subject.

Thanks also to Bláithín Connolly for modelling the pendants on page 114
and Daisy Barton for modelling the brooches on page 115.

While every effort has been made to credit contributors, Quarto would like
to apologise should there have been any omissions or errors – and would be
pleased to make the appropriate correction for future editions of the book.

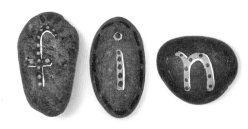